THE TWILIGHT
OF SOVEREIGNTY

THE TWILIGHT
OF SOVEREIGNTY

HOW THE INFORMATION REVOLUTION
IS TRANSFORMING OUR WORLD

WALTER B. WRISTON

CHARLES SCRIBNER'S SONS
New York

MAXWELL MACMILLAN CANADA
Toronto

MAXWELL MACMILLAN INTERNATIONAL
New York • Oxford • Singapore • Sydney

Charles Scribner's Sons   Maxwell Macmillan Canada, Inc.
Macmillan Publishing Company   1200 Eglinton Avenue East, Suite 200
866 Third Avenue   Don Mills, Ontario M3C 3N1
New York, NY 10022

Macmillan Publishing Company is part of the Maxwell Communication Group of Companies.

Library of Congress Cataloging-in-Publication Data
Wriston, Walter B.
The twilight of sovereignty: how the information revolution is transforming our world / Walter B. Wriston.
    p.   cm.
Includes index.
ISBN 0-684-19454-6
1. Information technology.   I. Title.
HC79.I55W75   1992
303.48'33—dc20   92-5069

Macmillan books are available at special discounts for bulk purchases for sales promotions, premiums, fund-raising, or educational use. For details, contact:

                Special Sales Director
                Macmillan Publishing Company
                866 Third Avenue
                New York, NY 10022

10 9 8 7 6 5 4 3 2 1

Printed in the United States of America

For Kathy

The world alters as we walk in it, so that the years of a man's life measure not some small growth or rearrangement or moderation of what he learned in childhood, but a great upheaval.

ROBERT OPPENHEIMER

CONTENTS

PREFACE

HISTORIANS LOOKING BACK ON EVENTS FROM THE PERSPEC-tive of many years often give names to eras that contemporaries living through those times never contemplated. Several hundred years passed before the eras we now know as the Middle Ages, the Renaissance, and the Reformation got their names. Today the case can be made that we do not have to wait for some future historian to name the age in which we are living: It is the Information Age. The evidence is plain to see everywhere around us. The world is now tied together by an electronic network that carries news and data, good and bad, true or false, with the speed of light anywhere on this planet. The massive amounts of information that move over the network, combined with the speed of transmission, are transforming the way the world works in ways at least as profound as occurred in the Industrial Revolution. It is changing the relationship between the government and the citizen; between one sovereign government and another; between corporations and regulators. The Orwellian vision of Big Brother watching the citizen has been stood on its head, and it is the citizen who is watching Big Brother. The perception of what constitutes an asset, and what it is that creates wealth is shifting dramatically. Intellectual capital is becoming relatively more important than physical capital. Indeed, the new source of wealth is not material, it is information, knowledge applied to work to create value. The pursuit of wealth is now largely the pursuit of information, and the application of information to the means of production. The sovereign's laws and regulations have not adjusted to the new reality. A person with the skills to write a complex software program that can produce a billion dollars of revenue can walk past any customs officer in the world with nothing of "value" to declare. An information economy also diminishes the rewards for control of territory and reduces the value of the resources that can be extracted through such control. Nation-states that fought bloody wars for the control of territory have often watched these conquered lands turn from an asset into a liability. Many of the natural resources contained within sovereign borders are being replaced by synthetics, which are basically the product of the mind. Borders once stoutly defended have become porous as data of all kinds move over, across, and through the lines on a map without let or hindrance.

Barbara Ward has observed that revolutions do not occur until people learn that there is an alternative to their way of life. In many parts of the world, all news contrary to the official line used to be tightly controlled. Information about other political systems was hard to come by. Today information about these alternatives is bouncing off satellites into hand-held transistor radios in remote jungles and moving across movie and television screens all over the world. The information technology, which carries the news of freedom, is rapidly creating a situation that might be described as the twilight of sovereignty, since the absolute power of the state to act alone both internally against its own citizens and externally against other nations' affairs is rapidly being attenuated. This does not mean that the nation-state will disappear; indeed, we will see more countries formed. But the message that is traveling on the network today, which is reshaping societies, was summed up by Baruch Spinoza in the seventeenth century: "The last end of the state is not to dominate men, nor restrain them by fear; rather, it is to set free each man from fear, that he may live and act with full security and without injury to himself or his neighbor. . . . The end of the state is really liberty." We have learned that freedom is a virus for which there is no antidote, and that virus is spread on the global electronic network to people in the far corners of the world who previously had no hope or knowledge of a better way of life. This process is in train and it cannot be reversed, since the technology on which it is based will not go away.

The path of freedom is never smooth, and there will be many reverses along the way, but in the words of the distinguished journalist Michael J. O'Neill, "Today's world cannot be remodeled with yesterday's memories: there are no U-turns on the road to the future." Yesterday there was no global network, but today the whole world understands its power. The protesters in Prague in 1988 understood it well as they chanted at the riot police: "The world sees you." And indeed it did.

This book grew out of the extremely good fortune I had to see the world from the perspective of a participant in the evolving global financial marketplace. The velocity of change we observed in every facet of life from health care to the weapons of war was driven by information technology of one kind or another. The monopoly of knowledge held by small groups was slowly broken down, with profound effects on society. It dawned on me that information, in the words of Leon Martel, was "rapidly replacing energy as society's main transforming resource."

As these ideas took shape, Bill Hammett, the president of a remarkable "think tank," the Manhattan Institute, encouraged me to undertake the task of writing this book and allowed the gifted editor of their magazine, *The City Journal*, Richard Vigilante, to work with me to bring order to the manuscript. His contribution was invaluable, and he has my profound gratitude. For more than twenty-five years Geraldine Stover has been able to read my handwriting and the somewhat less than perfect product of my word processor and turn them into flawless text; she has my thanks for outstanding stenographic support.

THE TWILIGHT OF THE IDOLS

The old order changeth, yielding place to the
new . . . lest one good custom should corrupt the
world.

ALFRED, LORD TENNYSON

D IPLOMATS, HISTORIANS, POLITICIANS, OR PHILOSOPHERS
rarely identify technological change as a decisive force in the
rise and fall of nation-states, preferring to explain the course
of history by the efforts of men and women like themselves.

In ancient Greece, Plato tells us, the leading men of the
city did not hold engineers in high regard: "You despise him
and his art," he wrote, "and sneeringly call him an engine-
maker, and you will not allow your daughter to marry his
son or marry your son to his daughter." Little has changed.

In today's world, many would have to concede that important technological breakthroughs may temporarily change the
military or economic balance of power. Even the most jaded
diplomat would agree that the balance of power in the world
altered decisively on July 16, 1945, on the desert of Alamo-
gordo, New Mexico, when the first atomic explosion took
place. Relations between nations were instantly altered, and
the very survival of our planet came into question. Yet many
of us assume that however much technology may alter the
means by which nations pursue their basic geopolitical in-

terests, those interests themselves will remain the same. This is not always the case.

The additive developments in science and technology that are often summed up in the phrase "the information revolution" are altering the shape and direction of national and international events in fundamental ways. We are witnessing a revolution in the relationships among sovereign states, in the relationships between government and citizens and between those citizens and the most powerful private institutions in society. And the "engine makers" are the leading revolutionaries.

The information revolution is profoundly threatening to the power structures of the world, and with good reason. The nature and powers of the sovereign state are being altered and even compromised in fundamental ways. The geopolitical map of the world is being redrawn. The elements of the balance of power that has prevailed for the last forty years have already been permanently disturbed and may soon be irretrievably altered or lost. Other institutions of our world, the business corporation chief among them, face equally powerful challenges to their modus operandi and will undergo profound changes that will affect all who are associated with them.

The information revolution, despite being the most frequently announced revolution in history, is still little understood. Many of the innovations that were trumpeted the loudest and earliest have never arrived: the checkless society, the paperless office, newspapers over cable TV, a helicopter in every backyard. Many of them may never arrive. But revolutions are not made by gadgets but by a shift in the balance of power. The underlying forces of the information revolution are causing such a shift in the balance of economic, political, and military power.

The information revolution is usually conceived, quite rightly, as the set of changes brought on by "information technologies," the two most important being modern communications technologies for transmitting information and modern computer systems for processing it. The marriage of these two technologies is now consummated. It is impossible to tell where communication stops and where computing begins. After years of study, in an attempt to determine which bureaucracy should have regulatory power, the federal government gave up on efforts to draw this distinction. In addition to powerful effects on culture and the pace of life, this revolution has changed what we do for a living. It has made many or most of us into what Peter Drucker long ago called "knowledge workers" and is changing the way the rest of us do such traditional jobs as mining and manufacturing, selling and shipping.

Most of us would probably be inclined to say that such dramatic changes are quite enough of an accomplishment for any revolution and that this one could retire from the field with a good day's work done. But underlying and driving the information revolution are two powerful tides that are rocking the power structures of the world: The first is the vast increase and swift and widespread dissemination of knowledge and of information of all sorts. The second is the increasing importance of knowledge in the production of wealth and the relative decline in the value of material resources.

From the beginning of time, power has been based on information. Someone learned to use a burning glass to start a fire; someone was able to find out where enemy troops were. Someone knew how to build a castle wall strong enough to withstand a siege, until someone else learned how to build a catapult or a cannon. Some politician found a pollster who gave notice of what the citizens really worried about. Timely information has always conferred power both in the commercial and the political marketplace.

The dissemination of once closely held information to huge numbers of people who didn't have it before often upsets existing power structures. Just as the spread of rudimentary medical knowledge took away the power of the tribal witch doctor, the spread of information about alternate life-styles

3

in other countries threatens the validity of some official political doctrines, the credibility of the leadership, and the stability of the regime.

The marriage of the computer with telecommunications, resulting in movement of information at the speed of light and to enormous audiences, tends to decentralize power as it decentralizes knowledge. When a system of national currencies run by central banks is transformed into a global electronic marketplace driven by private currency traders, power changes hands. When a system of national economies linked by government-regulated trade is replaced—at least in part—by an increasingly integrated global economy beyond the reach of much national regulation, power changes hands. When an international telecommunications system, incorporating technologies from mobile phones to communications satellites, deprives governments of the ability to keep secrets from the world, or from their own people, power changes hands. When a microchip the size of a fingernail can turn a relatively simple and inexpensive weapon into a Stinger missile, enabling an illiterate tribesman to destroy a multi-million-dollar armored helicopter and its highly trained crew, power changes hands.

The dictionary defines knowledge as the "acquaintance with facts, truths or principles, as from study or investigation." But knowledge can also be thought of as what we apply to work in the production of wealth. Knowledge is the ultimate source of value in work.

A rabbit running free through the meadow is not wealth. It becomes wealth as a resullt of information applied to the work of a hunter: information about where to find game, how to stalk it, how to throw a spear or shoot an arrow, how to make the arrow, the bow, or the spear. All these bits of information taken together and applied to the hunter's work produce value; that is, dinner for the hunter, his family, or the whole tribe.

Economists have a name for the work the hunter does to

turn rabbit into roast: value-added. Even in ancient days a considerable portion of that value-added was intellectual: the hunter's knowledge and skill. Nevertheless, in those days the bulk of the value-added was physical—long days in the field pursuing the rabbit, long and arduous efforts in shaping spear or bow, sharpening arrow or spearhead. And, of course, the original value in the deal was supplied by the rabbit, which fattened itself up in the meadow in pursuit of an agenda somewhat different from the hunter's.

Economic progress is largely a process of increasing the relative contribution of knowledge in the creation of wealth. The value of an ear of wild grain harvested by hunter-gatherers was almost entirely material, a gift of nature. Come the agricultural revolution and an ear of hybrid corn, grown in carefully fenced, rotated, fertilized, and irrigated fields, is to a very considerable extent the product of mind. The Industrial Revolution advanced the process further still as men greatly increased their capacity to manipulate matter and shape it to their needs.

In our time, the knowledge component of nearly all products has vastly increased in importance. As George Gilder has pointed out, the fundamental product of the information age, the microchip, the key component of all modern communications and computer technology, consists almost entirely of information. Raw materials represent about 1 percent of its costs; labor of the traditional sort accounts for another 5 percent. A majority of the cost—and value—comes from the information incorporated into the design of the chip itself and into the design and development of the highly specialized equipment used to manufacture it.[1]

The information technologies made possible by the chip have a profound effect on the rate of advance of all science, since calculations that used to take years can now be done in minutes. Scientific knowledge is currently doubling about every fifteen years. This vast increase in knowledge brings with it a huge increase in our ability to manipulate matter, increasing its value by the power of mind, generating new substances and products unhinted in nature and undreamed of but decades ago.

The effort to find, secure, and transport relatively rare natural resources—minerals, metals, coal, and oil—has been a key theme of economic production since the onset of the industrial age. Yet the value of all these materials is declining as the power of mind, enhanced by the intellectual hydraulics of information technology, is employed to replace them or economize on their use. Plastics replace metal and stone; fiber-optic cable replaces copper. Microchips are made from virtually worthless sand; superconducting ceramics, from common clay.

As computer-assisted calculations speed scientific investigations, so do they accelerate and simplify engineering and design. Better designs produce more efficient products, from airplanes to ovens, reducing energy needs and conserving on coal, oil, and other fuels. Indeed, prices of raw materials have been slumping worldwide for several decades, with only occasional and short-lived exceptions produced by OPEC (Organization of Petroleum Exporting Countries) or other political cartels.

The old industrial age is fading and being slowly replaced by a new information society. This transition does not mean that manufacturing does not matter, or that it will disappear, any more than the advent of the industrial age meant the disappearance of agriculture. What it does mean is that the relative importance of intellectual capital and intellectual labor will increase as that of physical labor and material capital declines. Knowledge applied to work has always created value, although many economists have tended to overlook its vital significance. In the world we are building, such an oversight will be increasingly difficult.

In sum, the world of work, the drama of economic production, the essential basis of our material existence, which for several centuries has been dominated by the brute forces of industry, is now dominated by products and processes that consist more of mind than of matter. These products and processes are faster and more mobile, have less need of centralized support, and are less dependent on natural resources, physical plant, or human labor than those of the recent past and thus are becoming far more difficult to regulate or control.

Sovereignty, defined by the *Dictionary of International Law* as "the supreme undivided authority possessed by a state to enact and enforce its law with respect to all persons, property, and events within its borders," is one of the most important ordering ideas of the modern world, a bulwark of modern power structures. Yet it is a relatively recent idea, first given to us in full-bodied form by the great Dutch jurist Hugo Grotius in his seminal work *De Juro Belli et Pacis* (Concerning the Law of War and Peace) in 1625. It is certainly possible to imagine a world in which state sovereignty as we know it did not exist or existed in substantially altered form.

As the dictionary definition implies, sovereignty has always been, in part, based on the idea of territoriality. The extent of a sovereign's reach has usually been defined by geographic borders. Even the immunities enjoyed by a foreign embassy are expressed in part geographically, by defining an area into which the host country may not intrude.

The control of territory remains one of the most important elements of sovereignty. But as the information revolution makes the assertion of territorial control more difficult in certain ways and less relevant in others, the nature and significance of sovereignty are bound to change.

As recently as World War II, armies fought and men died for control of the iron and steel in the Ruhr basin because ownership of those assets conferred real economic and political power. Today these once fought over assets may be a liability. To the extent that new technology replaces once essential commodities with plastics or other synthetic materials, the relative importance of these areas to the vital interest of nations is bound to change.

In 1967, Egypt closed the Suez Canal, and conventional wisdom told us that the lights would go out all over the world if this waterway between the Mediterranean Sea and the Gulf of Suez were ever closed. The power of a sovereign state, Egypt, to block the flow of oil to Europe was believed to be absolute short of war or other hostile action by the Western powers. The conventional wisdom did not take into account the technology that would allow the building of supertankers that could carry oil around the Cape of Good Hope economically. This feat was achieved by relatively simple technology, but it decisively altered the geopolitics of the Middle East. Similarly, advances in military technology are making once vital strategic "choke points" steadily less relevant. The velocity of change in economics, technology, science, and military capabilities is shifting the tectonic plates of national sovereignty and power.

One traditional aspect of sovereignty has been the power of nation-states to issue currency and mandate its value. Of course, the claims kings made for the worth of their currency did not always square with the facts. In the seventeenth century the Amsterdam bankers made themselves unpopular in the royal chambers by weighing coins and announcing their true metallic value. But those bankers spoke to a small audience, and their voices were not heard very far beyond the city limits. Despite the power of a righteous market, until very recently governments retained substantial power to manipulate the value of their currencies. As the information revolution has rendered borders porous to huge volumes of high-speed information, it has deprived them of that power.

The new international financial system was built not by politicians, economists, central bankers, or finance ministers but by technology. Today information about the diplomatic, fiscal, and monetary policies of all nations is instantly transmitted to electronic screens in hundreds of trading rooms in dozens of countries. As the screens light up with the latest statement of the president or the chairman of the Federal Reserve, traders make a judgment about the effect of the new policies on currency values and buy or sell accordingly. The entire globe is now tied together in a single electronic market moving at the speed of light. There is no place to hide.

This enormous flow of data has created a new world monetary standard, an Information Standard, which has replaced the gold standard and the Bretton Woods agreements.[2] The electronic global market has produced what amounts to a giant vote-counting machine that conducts a running tally on what the world thinks of a government's diplomatic, fiscal, and monetary policies. That opinion is immediately reflected in the value the market places on a country's currency.

Governments do not welcome this Information Standard any more than absolute monarchs embraced universal suffrage. Politicians who wish to evade responsibility for imprudent fiscal and monetary policies correctly perceive that the Information Standard will punish them. The size and speed of the worldwide financial market doom all types of central bank intervention, over time, to expensive failure. Moreover, in contrast to former international monetary systems, there is no way for a nation to resign from the Information Standard. No matter what political leaders do or say, the screens will continue to light up, traders will trade, and currency values will continue to be set not by sovereign governments but by global plebiscite.

The new global market is not limited to trade in financial instruments. The world can no longer be understood as a collection of national economies. The electronic infrastructure that now ties the world together, as well as great advances in the efficiency of conventional transportation, are creating a single global economy.

Commerce and production are increasingly transnational. The very phrase "international trade" has begun to sound obsolete. In the past, companies generally exported and imported products. On a national level, these transactions were aggregated and balanced according to the rules of a zero-sum game. Today this is no longer the rule. A product may have value added in several different countries. The dress a customer purchases at a smart store in New York may have originated with cloth woven in Korea, finished in Taiwan, and cut and sewed in India. Of course, a brief stop in Milan to pick up a "Made in Italy" label is de rigueur before the final journey to New York. Former secretary of state George Shultz recently remarked in a speech:

> A few months ago I saw a snapshot of a shipping label for some integrated circuits produced by an American firm. It said, "Made in one or more of the following countries: Korea, Hong Kong, Malaysia, Singapore, Taiwan, Mauritius, Thailand, Indonesia, Mexico, Philippines. The exact country of origin is unknown." That label says a lot about where current trends are taking us.

Whatever the correct word for these phenomena, "trade" certainly seems an inadequate description. How does one account in the monthly trade figures for products whose "exact country of origin is unknown"? How are national governments to regulate transnational production with anything like the firmness with which they once regulated international trade? How are politicians to whip up nationalist fervor against foreign goods when American car companies build cars in Mexico for export to Japan and pay the profits to pensioners in Chicago and the Japanese build cars in Tennessee for export to Europe and use the income to refinance real estate in Texas?

On the global business front, the new word is "alliances." Almost every day one reads about an American company and a Japanese company or a Swedish company and a German company—the list of combinations is endless—forming an alliance to offer a new product in a multinational horizontal integration of manufacturing, marketing, finance, and research. As these alliances grow and strengthen over time, it will become harder and harder for politicians to unscramble the emerging global economy and reassert their declining power to regulate national life.

The global market has moved from rhetoric to reality almost before we knew it. The old political boundaries of nation-states are being made obsolete by an alliance of commerce and technology. Political borders, long the cause of wars, are becoming porous. Commerce has not waited for the political process to adjust to technology but has tended to drive it. This is especially noticeable in Europe, where the new generation of business managers is bound and determined that the integration of the Common Market in 1992 will arrive on schedule, even though political leaders often seem reluctant to see their power compromised.

With national borders, sovereignty has traditionally entailed the government's power to regulate the leading enterprises of society, from health care to heavy industry. In an economy dominated by products that consist largely of information, this power erodes rapidly. As George Gilder has written, "A steel mill, the exemplary industry of the industrial age," lends itself to control by governments.

> Its massive output is easily measured and regulated at every point by government. By contrast, the typical means of production of the new epoch is a man at a computer work station, designing microchips comparable in complexity to the entire steel facility, to be manufactured from software programs comprising a coded sequence of electronic pulses that can elude every export control and run a production line anywhere on the globe.[3]

The information revolution not only makes the microeconomy more difficult to regulate; it makes the macroeconomy—

the world of gross national product (GNP) aggregate demand, and seasonally adjusted statistics—harder to measure and therefore harder to control. Many of the terms we use today to describe the economy no longer reflect reality. Everyone knows, for example, that all the lights would go out, all the airplanes would stop flying, and all the financial institutions and many of the factories would shut down if the computer software that runs their systems suddenly disappeared. Yet these crucial intellectual assets do not appear in any substantial way on the balance sheets of the world. Those balance sheets, however, do all reflect what in the industrial age were called tangible assets—buildings and machinery—things that can be seen and touched.

How does a national government measure capital formation when much new capital is intellectual? How does it measure the productivity of knowledge workers whose product cannot be counted on our fingers? If it cannot do that, how can it track productivity growth? How does it track or control the money supply when the financial markets create new financial instruments faster than the regulators can keep track of them? And if it cannot do any of these things with the relative precision of simpler times, what becomes of the great mission of modern governments? Controlling and manipulating the national economy? Even if some of these measurement problems are solved, as some surely will be, the phenomena they measure will be far more complex and difficult to manipulate than the old industrial economies.

The single most powerful development in global communities has been the satellite, born a mere thirty-one years ago with the launch of Sputnik. Satellites now bind the world, for better or worse, in an electronic infrastructure that carries news, money, and data anywhere on the planet at the speed of light. Satellites have made borders utterly porous to information. Geosynchronous satellites can and do broadcast news over curtains of iron, bamboo, or adamant government censors to anyone with a hand-held transistor radio.

One of the fundamental prerogatives assumed by all sovereign governments has been to pursue their national interests by waging war. Today this prerogative is being severely circumscribed by information technology. No one who lived through America's Vietnam experience could fail to understand the enormous impact that televison had in frustrating the government's objective in Southeast Asia. Knowing in a general way that war produces violent death is one thing, but watching the carnage of a battle or the body bags being unloaded at Dover Air Force Base on your living-room television set is quite another.

We have seen in the United States an organization publish the names of American agents in place overseas; we have read accounts in national newspapers detailing American naval and troop movements at a time of national emergency. Recently, a private company forced a superpower to change its policy. This occurred when the government monopoly on photographs from space was broken by the launching, in February 1986, of the privately owned French satellite SPOT. When the pictures of the Chernobyl nuclear disaster taken by SPOT appeared on the front pages of the world's newspapers, the Soviet Union was forced to change its story and admit that the event was much more serious than it had previously claimed. In this instance the technology was not new, but the power to use information shifted from the government to the private sector. The event posed a continuing dilemma: What SPOT revealed about Chernobyl, it can also reveal about American military sites. There is no American censorship of SPOT pictures as there had been on a de facto basis of photos taken from the American government's Landsat satellite.

While the resolution of SPOT's picture is only ten meters, it will undoubtedly be improved. The next logical development might be for an international news agency to purchase its own high-resolution satellite. Such a purchase would be a good deal less expensive, for instance, than the cost of covering the Olympics. If this happens, the guardians of national security will clash in space with the defenders of the First Amendment.

If democratic societies have difficulty adapting to what amounts to a whole new definition of sovereignty, closed societies, such as the former Soviet Union, will have a much more difficult time. Communist regimes have always based their power in part on their ability to control what their citizens see and hear. That control was seriously eroded by technology. News of the revolts in Eastern Europe was instantly relayed by radio and TV to the people of the former Soviet Union. The number of VCRs available in Moscow has been growing daily. Satellites are no respecters of ideology. Even the most draconian measures would be unlikely to halt the trend.

Nor can the former Soviet Union afford draconian measures. On the contrary, it faces an economic imperative to loosen controls further. Modern economies require access to huge amounts of information and the computer power to manipulate it. The free flow of scientific and technological knowledge is essential to innovation and continued productivity. Millions of researchers, scientists, and citizens in the United States now have access through their personal computers (PCs) to more than three thousand publicly available data bases, some storing billions of bits of technical, demographic, or scientific data. The former Soviet Union, in which information was the monopoly of the state and where even the GNP was a classified number, handcuffed itself. If the Kremlin wishes to keep pace with the West, it must allow its people to participate in the information revolution. But if it does so, it will lose an essential tool of state control. It is a Hobson's choice, and it will get more difficult over time. Indeed, history has resolved the dilemma with a swiftness that took all pundits by surprise.

The satellite, for all its power, is but a subset of a whole new class of "information weapons," weapons whose value is supplied largely by information technologies. As a rule, information weapons are equalizers that help small nations against large and favor defender over invader.

Perhaps the most dramatic current example is the use of the Stinger by the Mujahedin against the Russian invaders. The Stinger is one of the first truly "smart" missiles to be used extensively in battle. It has demonstated decisively that "artificial intelligence" can make a weapon costing but thousands of dollars, and affordable to even guerrilla armies, the superior of multimillion-dollar aircraft affordable in any considerable quantity only to the superpowers.

A less violent, but perhaps more destructive information weapon is the "software virus," dramatically illustrated in November 1988 by the invasion of a Department of Defense computer network by one such destructive program. Scott A. Boorman and Paul Levitt have argued that "with computer software now eighty percent of U.S. weapons system in development, attacks on the software . . . may be the most effective, cheapest, and simplest avenue to crippling U.S. defenses." Such sabotage may be within financial and technical reach of the smallest nations.

The challenge to national sovereignty poised by the information revolution is being replicated in various ways throughout most of the institutions of the modern world. In the business organization, the person who truly understands the impact of technology has become a vital part of the whole strategic business process. We see new corporate structures developing to manage new manufacturing methods, products, and delivery systems. Management structures are already changing dramatically. Layers of managements that used to do nothing but relay information from one level to another are beginning to disappear. Business is learning that these positions are no longer needed now that information technology allows the rapid transmission of vital information to all levels of management without human intervention. Instead, the old military mode of hierarchical organization is giving way to flatter structures designed for the faster response times needed to serve dynamic global markets.

A walk through a modern factory makes the point. Manufacturing plants are being run by computer hardware and software. The man with the clipboard who makes sure the widgets are in the right place on the shop floor at the right time is disappearing; the computer does it. The task of transmitting upward information on the state of the business is even more thoroughly automated. And more people in the system now have access to that information. Reports that used to take days or weeks to prepare, as well as the considerable support staff available only to senior management, are now available throughout the system at the stroke of a few computer keys. Plato wrote that democracy cannot extend beyond the reach of a man's voice, a limitation that provided a pretty good justification for the old system. In the new world, we may not see corporate democracies, but we will see the skills of the manager outstripped by the demand for leadership.

This sea change in our most important economic institutions (indeed in any of our great bureaucracies) will affect our daily lives and work in important ways. But as we shall see, the effects on society as a whole, while more subtle perhaps than those brought about by a revolution in the meaning and practice of national sovereignty, may be every bit as profound.

One of the recurring themes of history is our apparent inability to credit information that is at variance with our own prejudgments. Examples abound. The great historian Barbara Tuchman uses the Japanese attack on Pearl Harbor to illustrate the point. Though Japan had opened the Russo-Japanese War in 1904 by a surprise attack on the Russian fleet, American authorities years later dismissed the possibility of a similar maneuver.

We had broken the Japanese code, we had warnings on radar, we had a constant flow of accurate information . . . we had all the evidence and we refused to interpret it correctly, just as the Germans in 1944 refused to believe the evidence at Normandy. . . . Men will not believe what does not fit in with their plans or suit their prearrangements.[4]

This phenomenon, unfortunately, is not limited to discrete events. Few members of the current power structure wish to contemplate its decline, preferring to cherish the plans they have made, the strategies for victories economic, political, or military. But the contests for which they have faithfully prepared may never come, at least in the form expected, because the rules have been changed forever.

CHAPTER TWO

A NEW SOURCE OF WEALTH

> We might say that in the nineteenth century the
> wealth in California came from the gold in our
> mountains; today it comes from the silicon in our
> valleys.
>
> WILLIAM J. PERRY

DESPITE ALL THAT IS WRITTEN AND SAID ABOUT THE INFOR-
mation revolution, many people still have not faced how it
has changed the economy. While they understand that computers and telecommunications have become powerful economic forces, what many do not seem to realize is that these
technologies have done far more than speed up the industrial
economy or enrich it with new conveniences—or overload it
with new gadgets. The difference between the old industrial
economy and the new information economy is quantitative,
not merely qualitative. The world is changing not because
computer operators have replaced clerk-typists and can produce more work in less time but because the human struggle
to survive and prosper now depends on an entirely new source
of wealth; it is information, knowledge applied to work to
create value. Information technologies have created an entirely new economy, an information economy, as different
from the industrial economy as the industrial was from the
agricultural. And when the source of the wealth of nations
changes, the politics of nations change as well.

The Industrial Revolution changed the source of wealth, transforming once useless piles of rock and ore into riches of steel and steam. Even as it gave value to once neglected natural resources, industrialization dramatically increased the power of the nation-state not only by enhancing its revenues but also by expanding its regulatory power and the armaments needed to control those resources and the territory that embraced them. In the last few decades the information revolution is again changing the source of wealth, and even more dramatically. The new source of wealth is not material; it is information, knowledge applied to work to create value. The pursuit of wealth is now largely the pursuit of information and the application of intellectual capital to the means of production. This shift in perception of what constitutes an asset poses huge problems in expanding or even maintaining the power of government. Information resources are not bound to a particular geography or easily taxed and controlled by governments. A person with the skills to write a complex software system can walk past any customs officer in the world with nothing of "value" to declare. An information economy diminishes the rewards for control of territory and reduces the value of the resources that can be extracted through such control.

As a source of wealth, information comes in various forms, from streams of electronic data briefly valuable to years of accumulated research embedded in computer memories operating automated factories to the intellectual capital carried in the brain of an engineer, a manager, or an investment banker. The world desperately needs a model of economics of information that will schematize its forms and functions. But even without such a model one thing will be clear: When the world's most precious resource is immaterial, the economic doctrines, social structures, and political systems that evolved in a world devoted to the service of matter become rapidly ill suited to cope with the new situation. The rules and customs, skills and talents, necessary to uncover, capture, produce, preserve, and exploit information are now mankind's most important rules, customs, skills, and talents.

The information economy changes the very definition of an asset, transforms the nature of wealth, cuts a new path to prosperity. The information economy changes everything from how we make a living to how and by whom the world is run. The competition for the best information is vastly different from the competition for the best bottomlands or the best coalfields. Companies or nations competing for information will be vastly different from those that once competed primarily for material resources. The nature of information—how it is traded and produced, the scope, shape, and protocols of information markets, and the other institutions of an information economy—will impact government policy, set the limits of government power, and redefine sovereignty.

The changes in Eastern Europe are a dramatic example of the way the political structures are altered by information. The ideas, and even more important, the aspirations of the dissidents, rose on a flood of information, now flowing easily through what used to be called the Iron Curtain, about life in the West. Tactically, the revolution of 1989 made full use of modern communications technologies, from fax machines to satellite dishes to superlightweight video cameras and VCRs. But information played an even more important role in the Eastern bloc revolution. The *economic* power of information may explain the revolution's greatest mystery: why the Soviets and their satraps did so little to resist, and even encouraged, the changes. During the 1970s the Soviet economy—as it had for years—depended on gold, gas, oil, manpower, and military might, all of which were losing value compared to the resource in which, by idiotic political design, the USSR has long been poorest: information. As Gorbachev himself said: "The Soviet Union is in a spiritual decline. We have had to pay for this by lagging behind, and we will pay for it for a long time to come. We were one of the last to realize that in the age of information science the most valuable asset is knowledge—the breadth of mental outlook and creative imagination."

The Soviet leaders recognized that in an information economy only nations that allow information capital to flow freely will have enough of it to compete. The free flow of information, however, means liberating not only data but people and money, books and newspapers, and the proliferating electronic media. Free enterprise requires free expression. From the beginnings of *glasnost* Gorbachev's rhetoric showed that he grasped the price of a working modern economy. In 1991 he paid it.

The information revolution is one of the most heralded events in history, yet its essential nature is little understood. As everyone knows, the revolution was touched off, shortly after the invention of the electronic computer in 1946, by the remarkably rapid progress of computing and communications technologies. Over the past three decades, computers have grown in efficiency more than a millionfold. The computers of the fifties cost millions, required teams of expensive operators, filled whole suites of offices, were cumbersome to use or reprogram, and yielded but a fraction of the computing power of today's desktop personal computer (PC). In telecommunications the rise of fiber optics also enhanced efficiency as much as a millionfold. Today AT&T sends information between Chicago and the East Coast at the rate of 6.6 gigabits (the equivalent of a thousand books) per second. At this pace, the entire Library of Congress could be dispatched in twenty-four hours: Using conventional copper wire and a 2,400-baud modem it would take two thousand years.

In both technologies, progress was powered by the microchip, on which were integrated first dozens, then millions, of electronic switching circuits. Those switches are a computer's calculating tools and are also used by modern telecom systems—consisting largely of highly specialized computers—to compress and organize information and to speed up and direct its flow. Already the industry is placing some 10 million switches on a chip the size of a thumbnail. By decade's end, each chip will carry more than a billion switches, each operating in trillionths of a second.

These developments not only dramatically increased the computer's power to process and use information but radically decentralized that power by liberating computer users from the tyranny of the million-dollar mainframe. As late as the 1970s, Soviet economic planners were still devoting enormous resources to massive centralized computer systems by which they hoped to administer the entire Soviet economy without strangling it—the elusive Communist dream. The final collapse of those efforts was a crucial factor in the ensuing demoralization of the true believers and the rise and fall of Gorbachev. Meanwhile, in the free world, computing power was being spread throughout the economy by minicomputers, PCs, and workstations to liberate initiative and enable innovations impossible only a few years before.

These developments are as crucial as they sound. And yet they are not in themselves the information economy. The triumph of the information economy is seen not primarily in new things that are made of microchips but in the use of microchips to make the same old things out of a new resource: information. With but 2 percent of its costs attributable to energy and raw materials and but 5 percent to ordinary labor, the modern microchip is far more a product of mind than matter. The really remarkable thing about the microchip, however, is that it helps men and women turn nearly everything else they make into a product of mind and undermines every merely material advantage. The struggle to support human life in our unforgiving world still very much depends on making steel and concrete, building shelter, growing food, and moving resources from place to place. But now we build houses and offices and factories from information, we sow, fertilize, and harvest our crops with information, and we move our most precious—and some of our most common—possessions on highways of information.

Even steel, the paradigmatic product of the industrial age, has been transformed. A piece of steel, whether raw or as a part for a new automobile or skyscraper, is very different today from what it was a generation ago: It still contains a lot of iron mixed with other metals, but it contains a great deal more information. The extra information in modern steel would not show up dramatically in a chemical analysis— though hints of it are there in the subtly changing components of the alloy, and in some special steels, the lighter weight and greater strength of the metal. But in an economic analysis of modern steel the importance of information would resound from the figures. Modern steel plants use far less labor and energy, and even less raw material, to produce a given amount of steel than did the plants of a generation ago.

The biggest breakthrough in the steel industry in the past twenty years has been the "minimill," a new sort of steel mill using advanced melting, casting, and milling technologies. These technologies have freed steel making from its geographic ties to iron and coal deposits; have reduced capital costs for new mills by two-thirds; have reduced the minimum profitable size of a mill even more dramatically; and have doubled labor productivity. They have also, as we shall see, profoundly changed the lives of people who made their living from steel.

The minimill depends on electric rather than coal- or coke-driven furnaces. The electric furnace is not a new technology, but rapid improvements in the past few years have raised the quality and lowered the price of steel made in such furnaces. Electric furnaces primarily use scrap, which is cheaper and more abundant than raw steel, as their raw material. The huge "basic oxygen furnaces" used in the grand old integrated steel mills of the past cannot use much scrap without sacrificing quality. They must have raw steel, reduced from ore in hugely expensive blast furnaces, fed in their turn by massive coke ovens and ore processors. Because minimills do not depend on traditional raw materials, they can be located almost anywhere there is a market for a few hundred thousand tons of steel a year. Integrated mills had to be located near their raw materials or near huge ports to which those materials could be shipped and could be profitable only by turning out millions of tons annually.

Because they use electric furnaces, minimills can also use "continuous casters," which make basic steel shapes directly from molten steel. Old-style mills must first cast ingots, which are then premilled into basic shapes by expensive primary mills, before they can be sent to a rolling mill for final shaping. The continuous caster, like the electric furnace on which it depends, dramatically reduces both capital and labor costs.

These new technologies depend on an infusion of information into the steel-making process, a quantitative increase in the application of knowledge to work. They also depend significantly and increasingly on information technologies, particularly computers. Automated processing—the actual running of furnaces and mills by computers—was rather late coming to the steel industry but is now taking over the minimills, particularly those that make the most challenging and highest-quality products. The best continuous casters are computer driven; their processes are too precise for manual control.

Even before automation came to the mills themselves, computers were vital to the design and production of new steel-making technologies and equipment. To take a new steel technology from drawing board to working mill once required more than a decade. Now, with advanced computer modeling techniques eliminating much trial and error from the design process, a new idea can bear fruit in two or three years. Computer modeling has also reduced the amount of trial and error (and the waste in materials, labor, and money) mills undergo in meeting their customers' special needs for a particular run of steel.

Modern inventory control, accounting, and marketing procedures all rest on computer and telecom technologies. The greater strength per weight and volume of certain specialty steels is the result of our rapidly increasing scientific knowledge of the microstructure of materials, knowledge acquired in part by the application of computer power to research. "Computers change what we make, change how we make it, and change how we make the equipment to make it," says Donald Barnett, a leading expert on the steel industry and consultant to many of its most important companies.[1]

For all these reasons, a cost analysis of a given piece of steel would attribute a lot more value to information and information technologies, and a lot fewer to labor and materials, than was the case just twenty years ago. Steel is, as the philosophers might say, the limiting case. What is true for steel is even more true for the vast array of relatively traditional manufactured items that support our daily lives. For instance, even though steel is "smarter" than it used to be, newly invented plastic and composite materials containing an even greater proportion of information to matter are often substituted for it. Engineering advances, made possible by advanced computer modeling, make planes, trains, and automobiles far more fuel-efficient, thus substituting information for coal, oil, gas, and even more troublesome forms of matter, such as uranium.

Even in such a classically industrial enterprise as steel making, matter has become the enemy of wealth, not its source. As one might guess from their name, the outstanding feature of the minimills is that they are small—less matter goes into the making of them. That is also one key to their success. Their modest size, for instance, helps keep them technologically up-to-date. Because they require much less money ($15,000–$25,000 per employee) than traditional old-technology mills ($30,000–$45,000 per employee),[2] they can be profitable investments even with an economic life of only a decade or so and then be replaced with an even more advanced technology. Technology has helped reduce not only the minimum profitable capacity of a mill (to about two hundred thousand tons a year) but even the optimal capacity, from about seven million down to one million tons, making it far easier for modern mills to weather downturns in the economy.

Part of this innovation was driven by the instinct for survival as more and more steel was replaced by engineered plastics. Indeed, over the last ten years, not only has the consumption of steel in the United States not grown, it has turned negative. The trend in Europe and Japan is similar. These new plastics are themselves an example of applying information—in this case chemistry—to make a product that has already replaced a thousand pounds of steel on most of the world's automobiles.

By contrast, the massive integrated mills of the past were built to last indefinitely and on the assumption that basic steel technology would be as durable as the mills themselves. Pundits opine that the great American steel companies fell on hard times because management did not reinvest and rebuild as times changed. But this is untrue. During the 1970s the classic firms spent massively to expand capacity and, within the context of the old technology, to update their plants. No new integrated mills were opened, but many firms added considerably to their existing plants. The industrial age had taught them that increased scale would bring increased efficiencies, so they built huge new blast furnaces and coke ovens. Industrial economics had taught them that massive infusions of physical and financial capital would increase productivity, so they invested heavily in the most up-to-date, best-engineered, and most durable versions of an outmoded technology.

These classic strategies failed. In an information-rich economy innovations come quickly. The huge integrated steel plants were too big and expensive to adapt. Smaller plants are the easiest to automate; large plants can computerize only at great cost and without many of the efficiencies of smaller plants. Huge investments in industrial capital may even become a burden when information capital provides the competitive edge. Indeed, only two integrated mills have been built since 1950. In ten years, the big firms had lost much of their market and billions of dollars.

For all their ponderous mass, many of the old mills just disappeared. Their rusted hulks remain, undoubtedly to be sold as scrap to the minimills. But the essence of the huge mills—their massive capital investment, their great contribution to the nation's wealth, the 500,000 jobs and the communities that depended on them—are no longer anchored to the earth by the imperatives of matter and have floated away to other communities and other countries.

As the mills moved away or closed, tens of thousands of Americans saw their livelihoods and even their identities—as men who, by the labor of their bodies, had delivered their families to the safe harbor of the middle class—vanish as well. For a variety of reasons—including the great power of a union in a union town to which the company seemed bound by nature's distribution of iron and coal and the ports and loading docks to receive them—and its own massive investments, American steelworkers in the 1970s were paid twice the wage of the typical American industrial worker. But if the integrated steel maker could not leave town, steel making could. As the specialty and minimill technology developed, new mills were launched quickly and cheaply in towns that had never heard of the United Steel Workers and produced steel with two man-hours per ton versus three to six man-hours per ton in the old mills.

When steel mills can move to more hospitable climates, they no longer present a stationary target for government or union control. The more than sixty minimills in the United States moved not toward the coal and iron deposits in the ground but toward the source of scrap and cheap electricity. The new technology moved them into the information economy, not an economy of gadgets and computer games but a fundamental upheaval by which men and nations make their living and thus a revolution of all the rules by which we live.

Information has always been an important factor of production. The idea of substituting machines for manpower, for instance, is as old as the lever. It was the lever—in the form of a plow to turn the soil—that made agriculture possible. It was many years later that Archimedes boasted that given a lever long enough and a place upon which to rest it, he could move the earth. Of course no such lever existed, but by the thirteenth century a lever attached to a wheel produced the wheelbarrow, which did move the earth, albeit more gradually.

Until recently, however, even advanced manufacturing systems could make use of only small amounts of information. A few fairly simple instructions could be built into the mechanics of the system itself. The rest was carried around in the brains and on the clipboards and manuals of human operators. As for such questions as what to make, how to make it, what it should look like, when to schedule production, when to stock up on materials, when to draw down inventories, etc., that information was hardly integrated into the system at all. Information moved on myriad pathways and paper trails powered almost entirely by human beings, so-called service workers, who contributed mightily to the manufacturing enterprise.

Despite the intellectual achievements of the industrial age, information remained the most scarce and difficult to use of resources, which is why its use was minimized at every step. Thus, Henry Ford offered a Model T in any color the customer wanted as long as the customer wanted black: The cost of integrating into the system the information that 20 percent of customers wanted blue was too high for Ford's low-price strategy. When Alfred Sloan's innovations in corporate organization allowed General Motors (GM) plants to integrate rather modest amounts of marketing feedback into production decisions, GM became the leading carmaker, and Sloan went down in business history as a management genius.

Information technology is fundamentally different from industrial technology in that it can be programmed to do the required task and, if necessary, can be continuously adjusted. Industrial technology is just the opposite: The task must be adopted to the technology. It is a difference in kind and not just in degree. In the industrial economy, manufacturing systems were based on high volume, with sustained production runs producing standardized products. It usually took a long time—with the consequent shutdown of production—to change production runs. The new technology, however, permits the almost instant resetting of specifications, thus eliminating downtime. The garment trade is a good example of the new technology. The way in which the cloth is cut can be a high value-added operation or a money loser. It used to be that the great cutting machines had to be set up to cut only one size at a time, say, a size 8 regular, and the knife would slice through dozens of pieces of cloth at once to turn out fabric of the right size. If, however, the customer wanted a size 12 stout or some size 6 petites, it was a long and uneconomic job to reset the machine to turn out the odd sizes. Today, with computer-controlled cutters, the machine can be programmed to turn out any number of different sizes in any volume, thus making it economical to supply whatever the customer wants.

Although computers are thought of as operating in the service sector, they are now so integrated with manufacturing as to make separate categories useless. A walk through a modern factory makes the point. Manufacturing plants are now run by computer hardware and software that integrate huge amounts of information into the manufacturing process and process vast amounts of "feedback" information so as to make adjustments with a minimum of human intervention.

Digitally controlled machine tools are now linked together through communications systems and software to orchestrate entire production facilities. Human beings have found a way to apply their rapidly increasing knowledge to work to create value in ways unknown but a few years ago.

One innovation in this regard is the "expert system" by which modern technology is employed to capture knowledge so that it can continue to be applied to work and create value long after the person who acquired this valuable knowledge is gone. One famous expert system, used in GM factories, is called "Charley," after GM maintenance master Charley Amble, now retired. Charley the computer is an interactive system into which has been programmed the distilled wisdom of a lifetime of Charley Amble's experience in repairing machines. Over a period of twenty years Charley's job was listening to the noises machines make and, based on his analysis of the vibrations he heard, diagnosing whether or not the machine had to be adjusted, repaired, rebuilt, or retired. The vibration patterns of each machine are as distinctive as fingerprints, and their correct interpretation can save millions of dollars by timely preventive maintenance. His skill, experience, and rules of thumb, which had served him well, were painstakingly embedded in lines of software code. Today, even though the real Charley is gone, for the cost of $15,000, the price of a 50-megabyte workstation, an old factory's productivity is raised, and training time for maintenance people is greatly reduced. If the system cannot diagnose the trouble with certainty, it will offer a series of probabilities: a 60 percent chance the bearings are worn or a 70 percent chance that the alignment needs attention. Charley would be proud of the results.

Expert systems, artificial intelligence programs, computer-aided design, and computer-aided manufacturing systems are now used in major companies doing everything from process planning at aircraft plants to reformatting international payments at major money center banks around the world to designing and processing machine parts. All of these knowledge-based systems create value. They have become the essential component of industrial success.

In a newly automated General Electric (GE) locomotive plant in Erie, Pennsylvania, integrated information systems are weighted heavily toward the improvement of the management process itself. The system includes inventory control, order-entry systems, shop-floor reporting systems employing bar codes and wand-reading devices, payroll and accounting, master scheduling work, production control, job tracking, and more. Since 1984, the new systems have been largely responsible for increasing asset turnover by 50 percent. The combination of these management systems with newly automated machine tools on the factory floor has reduced by half the labor needed to make a locomotive. In an ironic footnote, it took some time for the new savings to turn into new sales. As GE chairman Jack Welch explains, the railroad companies have so improved their own efficiency by employing modern information systems that they need fewer locomotives. "Where they used to use 4,000 locomotives, they now carry the same amount of freight with 2,500."[3]

As information becomes the most important factor of production, there is less matter in nearly everything we make. From 1967 through 1988, the physical weight of U.S. product exports, per constant dollar value, fell 43 percent. The weight of U.S. imports fell even further.[4] Japan increased its industrial production two and a half times from 1965 through 1985 while barely increasing its consumption of raw materials and energy. As Peter Drucker has pointed out, the most important manufactured product of the 1920s, the automobile, owed 60 percent of its cost to raw materials and energy.[5] For the microchip that figure is only 2 percent, and for typical manufactured products today material and energy costs hover between 10 and 20 percent.

Labor also is being replaced by information. In the leading industrialized economies, workers today work only a bit more than half as many hours a year as they did in 1900, yet capacity of these economies to produce wealth has grown by at least twenty times since then. To manufacture a product in the United States in 1988 required, on average, only two-fifths of the blue-collar labor needed just eleven years earlier.[6]

Even factories are shrinking as machines get smaller, use less energy, and require fewer workers to tend them. Certain types of automated manufacturing systems have reduced by 60 percent the amount of floor space required to make a product compared to just a few years ago. Computer-coordinated, just-in-time production systems reduce inventory needs and waste. The average number of employees per factory, which rose steadily in the past, has been falling lately. The average U.S. factory employed fifty-one people in 1937 but only thirty-five people in 1982. These changes play out the central theme of the modern economy: to create value by putting more information into products and services or by taking matter out.

Virtually every society in history has believed that wealth flowed mainly from one form of capital, one type of productive activity, or one particular sector of society. Societies have often been wrong about the source of wealth, causing misery to themselves and others. But right or wrong, both a society's beliefs about the source of wealth and the underlying reality crucially affect political and social structures and the allocation of power.

For thousands of years men were nomads who attached themselves to herds of animals moving from pasture to pasture. Wealth was counted in the size of the herd. Men owned nothing that could not be carried. Land was not regarded as an asset, and its permanent control formed no part of the scanty political institutions of the day. When village agriculture began to appear, land became a form of wealth, as did water. Men began to lay down rules about the ownership of land and water rights, and political power began to shift away from nomadic chieftains and toward territorial rulers.

In the last years of the twentieth century it has been popular to say that real wealth comes from industry. Industry produces things that we can handle, things that are machined and solid, that we can see and touch. Only manufacturing creates real value by producing real goods for sale. Yet manufacturing itself was seen in an unfavorable light but a few hundred years ago. François Quesnay, the consulting physician to Louis XV and a founder of the so-called Physiocrat school of economics, argued that the source of all wealth was land. His disciples had a profound influence on many important figures, including Benjamin Franklin, who wrote that "agriculture is truly productive of new wealth; manufactures only change forms, and whatever value they give to the materials they work upon, they in the meantime consume an equal value in provisions."[7]

The cameralists, who powerfully influenced German policy in the late eighteenth century, postulated that there were three ways of increasing wealth: by increasing the population; by mining; and by controlling foreign commerce to produce an inflow of hard currency, which the state could hoard to pay for a huge army. Cameralist policies stifled German commerce, and Germany had to wait until the nineteenth century to become an explosive commercial power. Adam Smith published *An Inquiry into the Nature and Causes of the Wealth of Nations* in 1776 largely to dissuade the British Empire from mercantilism, which held that the state should firmly manage foreign trade for apparent national advantage. In arguing for the freedom of commerce, Smith showed that the ingenuity of British workers and businessmen was worth more than the hoards of gold in the king's treasure houses.

Smith's daunting task was to convince the ever more powerful sovereigns of his day to relinquish some of their cherished powers over trade and production for the good of their people and thus increase the rulers' own wealth. The emergence of the information economy will require concessions of sovereign authority far greater than those Smith asked of the English Crown.

Sovereignty is a modern institution but a few hundred years old, though like many modern institutions it began as a medieval idea, arising out of the efforts of kings to break the power of feudal lords and city-states and remove the privileges of the Church and trade guilds. By the nineteenth century, sovereignty came to mean that power by which a sovereign was empowered to act alone, without the consent of any higher authority. In international affairs, a state is sovereign if in the ordinary course of events its decisions are not legally or customarily reviewable by any other state.

In a modern sovereign state there may be many social and economic institutions that compete with the state for power—churches, universities, corporations, voluntary associations—and some of them may be powerful. Yet all such institutions live and act at the sufferance of the sovereign. Even in as liberal a nation as the United States, for example, the churches are free of government control not by virtue of ancient historical right or the force of custom or a commonly accepted view of natural law or the divine will or the protection of a rival sovereign or the churches' own economic, political, or military power but by the sovereign's own law, as expressed in the First Amendment.

Few modern states have been as sovereign as classical theory implies, in large part because of the power of these private institutions. Though the institutions are never any match for the state in raw power, their utility, popularity, or prestige has generally won them some degree of autonomy from the state. Nevertheless, the broad drift of political history since the waning of the Middle Ages has been toward sovereignty.

The emergence of information as the preeminent form of capital reverses this drift toward centralizing power. The nation-state will not disappear; indeed, we will see many new nations formed. Nor will sovereignty vanish either as an idea or as an institution. But the power of the state will diminish, particularly its sovereign power: the power to judge without being judged, to delimit the powers and privileges of the other institutions within society. Even Japan, which for years appeared to be in firm control of its own destiny, is seeing market forces overwhelm its bureaucratic power. After World War II, the powerful Japanese Ministry of International Trade and Industry (MITI) proposed that Japan's twelve automobile companies merge to create two or three companies to battle America's Big Three. Instead, the Japanese auto companies defied the powerful MITI, and Toyota and others refused to specialize in cars of a certain size and became market driven to produce a full line of cars the customer wanted.

Information has always been power; now it is also wealth. Nonmaterial and, with the aid of modern technology, extremely mobile, information can escape government control far more easily than other forms of capital. Draconian or even merely bureaucratic systems for controlling the flow or use of information tend to destroy or waste it. Economically useful information is usually original, innovative, or at least timely, nuanced, precise, complex, and challenging. Bureaucracies and governments live for delay, blunt originality, oppose innovation, abhor nuance. Governments are good at governing matter but everywhere misrule mind, especially the best and most productive minds, minds that are frustrated and demoralized by the pretensions of the merely powerful.

Governments are good at regulating, taxing, confiscating, and controlling things that they can readily see, measure, and keep track of, things that don't readily move out of town or across the border and cannot be concealed inside a man's head. Governments have always sought to exact high "rents" both in the form of taxes and other government controls from businesses located within their borders. Such rents are a very important source of government power and wealth. In an information economy, government rent collectors have much less leverage because the tenants can leave town.

In the industrial era, progress was built on massive economies of scale, which made capital easy to exploit. As firms, plants, and machines got larger, they became more difficult to move in the event of government harassment or expropriation. To Karl Marx this immobility seemed an opportunity: It was possible in those days to imagine that the state really could capture the capital assets of society and manage them for the good of the proletariat—or the *nomenklatura*. This did not often happen, and certainly not in the way Marx imagined. But the great leverage governments held against nearly captive capital—mines and land, forests and factories—did allow and promote an enormous expansion of government power. As long as capital consisted largely of factories, heavy equipment, and natural resources, governments felt free to impose rules and exact payments with no fear that the nation's capital base would steal away in the night. Extreme impositions would reduce productivity—the Communist economies never worked very well—but on the whole, government held the cards.

All this has changed. Intellectual capital will go where it is wanted, and it will stay where it is well treated. It cannot be driven; it can only be attracted. Its movement across borders or around the world cannot be stopped, and even the most totalitarian governments can do no more than temporarily impede it. As Gorbachev discovered, states that impose exorbitant rents on information enterprises, either in taxes, regulation, or simply in political control and repression, soon will not have enough information capital to compete. Such societies are generally run by people who simply do not understand the power of information capital or the workings of a modern economy; if they had understood, they would not have imagined that police and military might could build or sustain a nation. The economic history of Eastern Europe stands witness to this truth.

Under the strain of global competition for information capital, governments are more likely to reduce rents than raise them. They will compete to cut taxes and deregulate—as most of the industrialized and industrializing nations have been doing for more than a decade—and they will knock down the Berlin Wall. Not all governments will move at the same speed; Tiananmen Square is but one reminder that the record is not and will not be perfect. We are speaking of a political trend, not a law of physics; but in politics, powerful trends are made by slight changes in what the Soviets used to call the "alignment of forces."

When natural resources were the dominant factor of production, the conquest and control of territory seemed a reliable way to enhance national power. Today conquest of territory is rarely worth the cost to the nation. War and long years of pacification and repression almost inevitably destroy or scatter intellectual capital, and the material resources that might be gained by conquest are everywhere declining in value. Size can still be an advantage—the United States will probably always be a greater power than Singapore—but imperialist adventures now have a far higher "hurdle rate of return."

The information economy, as we shall see in greater detail later, is intractably global. In part this is because trade in information, now little bound by geography or burdened by matter, is global. A truly global economy, as opposed to the multinational economy of the recent past, will require concessions of national power and compromises of national sovereignty that seemed impossible a few years ago and which even now we can but partly imagine. Such an economy cannot be readily contained or controlled by mercantilist or protectionist strategies. The attempts of sovereign states to cut off and control little bits of the world market for their own advantage will be more obviously futile than ever in the past. And yet control of international trade has been one of the most cherished of sovereign powers since well before the Industrial Revolution.

People who carry in their heads an increasing amount of intellectual capital also pose a challenge to government, since if the nation is to prosper, governments must court and keep their human resources. Increasingly, their specialized knowledge will make them more difficult to govern. In many areas of economic and social life in which the government once credibly professed to be the only party both sufficiently qualified and disinterested to lay down the rules, "knowledge workers" will rightly feel themselves better informed than government regulators. Government intervention, once the cherished protection of weaker parties, will be increasingly resented and opposed by an ever larger class of such workers. These citizens are a new bourgeoisie who carry the means of production in their brains. Unlike Marx's bourgeoisie, their power and numbers are destined to grow, not decrease. And they are unlikely to view the government as a natural ally.

Nowhere will the power of these knowledge workers be more evident than in those great nongovernmental institutions whose subordination to the state is essential to sovereignty as we have known it. As Drucker writes:

> Theory still postulates that there is only one organized power center—the government. But both society and polity in developed countries are now full of power centers that are outside of and separate from government. Each of these institutions has to have a great deal of autonomy to produce results.[8]

As even the Communist nations seem finally to have learned, subjecting business organizations—including nonprofit business, such as hospitals and schools—to the control of a large central government bureaucracy is not a recipe for success.

These private institutions began their rapid increase in size and power long before the computer era. The growth of the great modern private organizations dates from about the midpoint of the Industrial Revolution and was prompted by the need to organize human efforts on a scale rarely attempted outside the army. In the information economy, these institutions become relatively far stronger thanks to the information capital that uniquely suits them to their tasks. Those tasks become more demanding and specialized, making it harder for any generalist, including those who run the government, to supervise their work without stymieing it. The people who dominate these institutions—even when they do not formally run them—are professionals, treated by their own supervisors not as subordinates but as colleagues. They do not respond well to old "command and control" styles of management, nor do they have to: They are conscious of their value. The transformation of General Electric from a huge bureaucracy to a company where the people on the shop floor are the ones whose ideas are not only heard but implemented has turned out to be the premier example of this phenomenon. What is true for the inhabitants of these institutions is true for the institutions as a whole. The information economy increases these institutions' need for autonomy as well as the intellectual and economic leverage by which they procure this autonomy.

CHAPTER THREE

THE GLOBAL CONVERSATION

> In the early years after the Russian revolution, Leon
> Trotsky reportedly proposed to Stalin that a modern
> telephone system be built in the new Soviet state.
> Stalin brushed off the idea, saying, "I can imagine
> no greater instrument of counterrevolution in our
> time."
>
> WILSON P. DIZARD AND S. BLAKE SWENSRUD,
> *Gorbachev's Information Revolution*

THE PHILIPPINES HAS MANY COLLEGE GRADUATES AND NOT always enough jobs for them. Until recently they faced a hard choice: emigrate to a place where they can profit from their skills or stay home in relatively menial, low-paying jobs. Today they enjoy a new option. Stay at home and export the products of their minds over the electronic infrastructure of the global economy. Several U.S.-based Big Six accounting firms, for instance, now perform computer-assisted audits for American clients using customized software programs written by Filipino programmers and shipped via satellite back to the States. For some jobs the raw financial data are put on-'ne and shipped to the Philippines, where the books are au-'ed half a world away from company headquarters.

'he Philippines is not unique. Indian programmers write ons of lines of code for such companies as American s for use in data centers. Meanwhile, construction and ring firms are using computer-assisted designs made ı to build structures anywhere in the world. All of this work is done by skilled labor that has no occasion to apply for an immigration visa or a green card.

Geography and local conditions no longer condemn the intellectual resources of the provinces to chronic underemployment. Immigration quotas that bar physical travel have no effect on intellectual capital, since virtually the entire globe is bound together by an electronic delivery system—including not only a revolutionized telecom system but a global network of satellite and broadcasting technologies, electronic markets, and VCRs—through which information, news, and money move from place to place with astonishing ease and speed.

This new electronic superhighway can transform the livelihood of a farmer in a small village on a faraway island nation or handle in a single day an exchange of financial assets that exceeds the gross national product (GNP) of most of the countries in the world. Telephones were only recently installed in several Sri Lanka villages. Until then, farmers had sold their produce to wholesalers for but a fraction of its market value in the capital city of Colombo. After the telephone came, the farmers always knew the prices in the city market and increased their income by 50 percent.[1] Even such a simple manifestation of the power of a telecom network can change economic destinies and may start a train of political events of immense consequence.

The very same network in the past few years has revolutionized the way the world's money is traded. As late as 1973 the world money market, such as it was, resembled a giant telephone bee. Groups of traders sitting around banks of black telephones would dial up other traders or brokers with their bids and offers, laboriously shopping for the best deal. No matter how industrious the traders were, they saw only a small part of the market. In 1973 this all changed when Reuters replaced those black telephones with a video terminal, called Monitor, that assembled bids and offers from banks and trading rooms all over the globe, displaying them on request for everyone on the system to see, thereby creating the first true global money market. Reuters and similar services provided by other companies have wrought a greater transformation in world financial markets in fifteen years than those markets had undergone in the previous centuries. As recently as 1980, the daily volume of trading in the foreign exchange market in the United States was estimated at only $10.3 billion. By 1989, this total had grown to an average of $183.2 billion per day.[2] And the U.S. market is but one part of a global market, albeit a substantial one.

The telephone has been around for more than a century, and radio and television for several generations, so it is easy to imagine that the new network is not new at all and represents nothing more than a marginal, if significant, enhancement of an institution long assimilated to the economic and political structures of the world. Nothing could be further from the truth. The new global network is a radical innovation, fundamentally changed not only in quantity but quality from the system of but twenty years ago. Since our legal system is based on the written word, the telephone was viewed with some skepticism by governments and courts. The question of whether or not an oral contract, if made by telephone, was valid took years to adjudicate. Today foreign exchange contracts of up to one year—absent fraud—are routinely binding. To guard against fraud, every trading room keeps a record on tape of all conversations over the network so that there can be no dispute about what was said.

Practically speaking, even ordinary international telephone service—regular voice lines, nothing fancy—is barely more than a generation old. The first transatlantic cable capable of carrying telephone voice transmissions was not laid until 1956. It could carry a grand total of thirty-six very expensive conversations at one time. Quality was frequently poor, too poor for transmission of complex nonvoice messages, such as the computerized data used by electronic money markets.

Moreover, data transmission uses much more cable capacity than does voice; in 1956, any attempt to move data on transatlantic cable would have quickly clogged every available line.[3]

In the 1950s and 1960s the difficulty of getting a telephone connection from Citibank headquarters in Brazil to world headquarters in New York was monumental. There were so few international lines available that it could take a day or more to get a circuit. Once a connection was made, people in the branch would stay on the phone reading books and newspapers aloud all day just to keep the line open until it was needed. The local situation was hardly better. Citibank had to hire squads of Brazilian youths, whom we called dialers, who did nothing but dial phones all day in hope of getting through.

It was not possible to build a truly global economy under such conditions. The global information economy lives on the phone: In all the leading industrialized economies telephone density now approaches one telephone per person. Yet as recently as the mid-1960s, France, West Germany, Italy, and Japan all had fewer than fifteen phones per hundred people. An American tourist might have been surprised to discover that his Naples hotel room lacked a phone or that a French acquaintance's only home telephone was the public one on the street corner. Today over 100 million telephone calls, utilizing some 300 million access lines, are completed worldwide every hour. It is estimated that the volume of phone transactions will triple by the year 2000.[4] As late as 1966, the transatlantic cable could still handle only 138 conversations between all of Europe and all of North America at any one time.

Then came a dramatic series of technological developments. In 1966 a new and vital satellite link in the global net was positioned in a geosynchronous orbit over the Atlantic. At an altitude of 22,000 miles above the equator, satellites take exactly one day to complete a revolution and so remained fixed over the same spot on earth. As both governments and private companies developed better use of the electromagnetic spectrum, the capacity of satellites has increased by a factor of about forty-five and counting. Meanwhile, back on earth we were still practicing a nineteenth-century concept of sovereignty expressed in a statute passed by Congress on May 27, 1921, mandating "that no person shall land or operate in the United States any submarine cable directly or indirectly connecting the United States with any foreign country . . . unless a written license to land or operate such cable has been issued by the President of the United States. . . ."

While the president contemplates the wisdom of issuing a license, his country is "connected" to every "foreign country" by myriad channels over which he has little, if any, control.

In 1976, the sixth transatlantic cable was laid. Using new technologies, it could carry four thousand conversations at once, a real breakthrough in capacity. The first fiber-optic transatlantic cable, laid in 1988, could carry forty thousand conversations at once.[5] In the early 1990s the world will have almost a million and a half voice-capable intercontinental circuits at its disposal.[6]

A hefty portion of those circuits travel via geosynchronous communications satellites, which in the past twenty years have become an essential part of the world communications infrastructure. Other crucial technological advances include dramatic increases in cable capacity and switching efficiency and sophistication. Fiber-optic cable, which bears light impulses over "glass" fibers, can carry far more information than copper wires bearing streams of electrons. Electronic switches—essentially specialized computers—replaced the old mechanical arrays, cutting costs, increasing capacity, and facilitating "multiplex" switching, the practice of sending several conversations over the same circuit simultaneously.[7]

This completely new telecom system has already made a global market in such easily digitized phenomena as money and securities, computer programs and engineering designs. But the combination of the new global telecom system with advances in other communications media is creating a world market not only in every other sort of economic product and service but in culture and entertainment, fashion, and even government. It has made a reality of Marshall McLuhan's global village by drawing nearly all the world into a single global conversation, one that now assesses, approves, and disapproves globally products and services, institutions and ideas, that once were evaluated primarily on local markets.

Markets are voting machines; they function by taking referenda. In the new world money market, for example, currency values are now decided by a constant referendum of thousands of currency traders in hundreds of trading rooms around the globe, all connected to each other by a vast electronic network giving each trader instant access to information about any factor that might affect values. That constant referendum makes it much harder for central banks and governments to manipulate currency values.

In the same way, modern communications technologies, including the vast expansion of the telecom network, VCRs, electronic data bases, ever cheaper and simpler techniques for collecting and broadcasting the news, and the fax machine, are creating a global market that takes constant referenda on what in many ways is beginning to look like a global culture. While hundreds of thousands of financial specialists now have instant access to economic and financial news, hundreds of millions of people around the world are plugged into a single network—albeit with local interests and subdivisions—of popular communication. All of a sudden, everyone has access to everything. CNN is available to a huge portion of the world's population. Tens of millions of Chinese and Indians, Frenchmen and Malays, are watching "Dallas" and the "Honeymooners," which in their way may be more subversive of sovereign authority than CNN. The people plugged into this global conversation are voting—for Madonna and Benetton,

Pepsi and Prince—but also for democracy, free expression, free markets, and free movement of people and money. Indira Gandhi is said to have remarked that in the Third World a revolution could be started when a peasant glimpsed a modern refrigerator in a TV sitcom, a remark that almost perfectly sums up the power of the global culture market.

This market, of billions of plugged-in "culture traders," is now the most powerful social and political force in the world. It is at the heart of the breakup of communism and the unification of Europe. The fear of the global culture market is one of the powerful motives behind the emergence of the Islamic republics and their desperate drive to cut their people off from modernity.

Not everyone is fully plugged in to the global conversation or equipped to take full advantage of it. Those who fully participate in the information economy benefit most from it. The global network is the essential infrastructure of that economy, and its use promises to make its users into a single worldwide community sharing many tastes and opinions, styles of dress, forms of government, and modes of thought. These people, on the whole, will be internationalists in their outlook and will approve and encourage the worldwide erosion of traditional sovereignty. They will feel more affinity to their fellow global conversationalists than to those of their countrymen who are not part of the global conversation. These latter will have little at stake in the global conversation and may come to hate it and those who participate in it as they realize that in all this talk they are rarely mentioned and then only as a social problem. All technological progress has created social problems, and the information revolution moving over the global network is no exception. New skills and new insights will be required to survive and prosper, and those who do not or cannot adapt will be left behind with all the social trauma that entails.

The global network is also both a temptation and a nemesis for governments. Yet it is the one path to prosperity in the global information economy. Now that there are global markets in money, in information capital, in a steadily growing portion of the world's products and services, and even in human intellect—all utterly dependent on the new world communications network—no nation can hope to prosper in the future unless it is fully hooked up to the network and its citizens are free to use it.

A nation can walk this path to prosperity only if its government surrenders control over the flow of information. In the world we are building today it is almost impossible to assert sovereignty over information because information and the pathways over which it travels, including the heavens themselves, are shared in common. The sovereign can, at enormous cost, cut his nation off from some of those shared pathways by shutting down the international phone circuits or shooting anyone caught with a fax machine, a radio, or a tiny satellite dish. Even then he cannot succeed entirely. When he is finished, he will be ruler of Albania.

Fax machines and computer-driven telephone switches came to China because the Chinese rulers wanted a modern economy; within months they became an infrastructure of revolution. That revolution was brutally suppressed, but the leadership has not found—and never can find—a way to build an information economy in a closed society.

In the West we are well used to a free market in public attention: Publishers, producers, and politicians all know that they must persuade the audience to lend its ears and eyes, which means giving the audience what it wants. This may not always be good for high culture, but the competition of ideas makes a propagandist's life difficult.

Recently a young Chinese filmmaker made a documentary about the Chinese army that found its way onto cable TV. The film shows exhilarating and terrifying scenes of a tank division training in Mongolia—impressively uniformed and disciplined troops responding to the call to battle, mounting their tanks and getting a division on the roll, it seemed, in a matter of minutes. But the very next scene shows the same troops, now stripped down to T-shirts and fatigues, their change in costume revealing them as teenage boys, break dancing to American music blasting from a boom box. How well can patriotic indoctrination work when it faces such open competition from competing entertainments? It has been said that the sixties generation sang America out of Vietnam. Will Chinese soldiers dance their way out of the next Tiananmen Square?

Satellites have been perhaps the principal force in altering the "balance of information power," tipping it away from the state and toward the individual. Until 1986, Landsat, with its thirty-meter resolution, offered the only commercially available photographs from space. Then there was the launching in February 1986 of the privately owned French satellite SPOT, with a ten-meter resolution. The Russians then entered the fray by offering to sell to anyone with the cash their best-quality imagery with a five-meter resolution. The U.S. government was forced to reverse its policy and permit American private companies to own high-resolution satellites. This in effect removed the de facto censorship of the photos taken by Landsat and loosened one more sovereign prerogative. It is not beyond the realm of possibility for American or other news agencies to purchase their own high-resolution satellites; indeed, it would be a good deal less expensive than covering the Olympics.

Satellite communications, combined with innovations in video recording technology, are turning the entire world into a local news beat. Until the mid-1970s no one had ever heard of "minicams," the relatively inexpensive portable video cameras that record sound and picture on a tape cassette. Minicams can and do go anywhere and have eliminated cumbersome cables, thousands of pounds of equipment, and the time needed to process film and transfer it to tape. Equally important has been the advent of the mobile satellite hookup, by which a portable camera, linked by but one cable to a mobile video truck, can send sound and picture first to a local TV station and from there to a satellite and around the world.[8]

These two technologies have dramatically speeded and expanded television reportage. In the 1970s fewer than half of all television news stories were shown on the day they happened. Today, except for in-depth "magazine" features, nearly all news is broadcast the day it is taped. In the early 1970s it cost $4,000 to get a line to send television material from Seattle to New York. Today, by satellite, it costs about a tenth as much. Governments could once count on knowing more about sensitive international events than their citizens. Now they often find themselves following those events on television. A CNN monitor sits in the corner of all government crisis-management centers of the U.S. government.

Satellites have also vastly increased the reach of television broadcasts and made it so difficult for governments to interdict suspect programming that many of them have stopped trying. CNN is now carried to one-third of the earth's surface by a Soviet-built and controlled satellite.[9] It was available, relatively freely, in the Soviet bloc even before the revolutions of 1989.

In fact, incoming Western broadcasts reassured the dissidents in Eastern Europe that the world was following their struggles and helped them focus and amplify their message. Even state-controlled news broadcasts, in an attempt to retain their credibility and their audience, became steadily more candid. All these factors were crucial to the events of 1989. As Timothy Garton Ash, a prominent English journalist who recorded the Eastern European revolutions of the 1980s, has written: "Both externally and internally, the crucial medium [of the revolution] was television. In Europe at the end of the twentieth century all revolutions are telerevolutions."[10]

Despite the over-the-air broadcasts, the Ministry of Truth's toughest competitor in the global culture market may be the VCR. These machines and the tapes that play in them have been licensed, restricted, regulated, taxed, censored, and even banned by so many countries so vigorously that the campaign against them makes the history of print censorship seem like an ACLU (American Civil Liberties Union) workshop. Nevertheless, in almost every country in the world, including the Soviet Union and the Islamic republics, people have easy access to machines and tapes and can watch almost whatever they choose.[11] Vigorous competition from VCRs is clearly weakening state control of broadcast television. Western movies or TV series get better audience share than endless speeches from the leader or hygienic dramas. In the early 1980s, East Germany began to show Western films so as to compete with both VCRs and West German TV. In Tanzania, which has long suffered under a particularly draconian form of socialism administered by Julius Nyerere, television was banned altogether for years, though people did tune in to foreign broadcasts on illegal sets. When VCRs came on the scene, illegally, they proved too popular for the government to control. Within a few years the government relented, lifting the ban on VCRs and permitting people to receive foreign broadcasts on their TVs.

These machines can also have more direct and explosive political effects. Within days of the 1983 murder of Benigno Aquino, the long-outlawed and exiled political rival of Ferdinand Marcos, the Philippines was flooded with smuggled videotapes of the assassination at Manila International Airport. At least one of the original tapes was smuggled in camouflaged as a pornographic film. Philippine TV and press coverage of the assassination had omitted video footage implicating Filipino security forces in the murder. The smuggled tapes carried that footage as well as investigative reportage from news organizations around the world linking the Marcos government to the murder. The tapes did much to arouse the Filipino middle class, until then fairly complacent, against the Marcos regime, demonstrating that apparent control of the nation's broadcast system no longer protects governments from the power of the video image.

Once a nation is linked to the network, it is very difficult for its rulers to control how the network is used. Stories of electronic surveillance in the now dismantled Soviet bloc are common enough. But in reality the former Soviet government suppressed the flow of information not by tapping everyone's phones but by keeping most people from having them. The Soviet phone system is dismal. Even in the cities only 23 percent of Soviet homes had telephones in 1985; in rural areas the figure was 7 percent. Even many state-operated facilities, such as collective farms and rural hospitals, had not a single phone. It can take hours or days to make a domestic long-distance call; international circuits are scarce, expensive, and restricted, with only fifty lines to the United States as late as 1987.[12]

There is no greater proof of the tremendous economic importance of plugging into the global network—and of building an adequate version thereof at home—than the risks the Russians now seem willing to take to rectify this situation, thereby surrendering what had been a linchpin of Soviet power for three generations. According to official figures, Russian telecom expenditures are increasing by double-digit percentages. The government has established a goal of having 90 million phones, or one for every three people in the nation, by the end of this century. In part this growth is required by the decision to move in the direction of the market economy. As centralized planning is replaced with networks of market relationships, factories, suppliers, distributors, retailers, and their computers will have to be able to talk to each other.

When everyone in the nation, at least potentially, can join in a single national conversation, there are only two ways in which a government can maintain its power: It can allow its policies to be guided by that national conversation and so keep the confidence not only of "the people" but also of the bureaucrats and the army. But a government that consents to be so guided has become in some sense, however attenuated, democratic and is likely to keep moving in that direction.

The other way to keep power is to revert to a level of repression that even totalitarian regimes find inconvenient, that in an age of instant information brings world opprobrium, and that over time will guarantee economic, technical, and—finally—military decline.

The control of information is the bedrock of all totalitarian regimes. The Soviets for decades devoted enormous resources to control radio and television, printing presses, photostat machines, and even mimeograph machines. Certainly some information—political ideas, news about life outside the Iron Curtain, et cetera—always circulated within the USSR. But neither the volume of the information nor the freedom of its circulation was great enough to support any coherent resistance—even peaceful resistance within the Party—to Communist dogma. As a Russian émigré friend once strikingly told me: "It is quite possible for an entire country to know it is being lied to and yet not have any clear or useful idea of what the truth might be."

Now it is much more difficult to sustain the lie. That is the key to the events of 1989. Though Communist ideology had long lost its moral and intellectual power, as late as the 1980s people were required to pay public obeisance to it, with the result that nearly everyone was leading a double life, saying one thing in public and another in private. However the people of Eastern Europe might have despised the public lie and their own complicity in it, that lie still blocked a candid national conversation, "the public articulation of shared aspirations and common truths," as Garton Ash puts it. That is why public witness to the truth was so critical to the revolution, why words defeated tanks:

> As they stood and shouted together, these men and women were not merely healing divisions in their society; they were healing divisions in themselves. Everything that had to do with the word, with the press, with television was of the first importance to these crowds.

The semantic occupation was as offensive to them as
the military occupation; cleaning up the linguistic environment as vital as cleaning up the physical environment.[13]

The implications of the global conversation are about the
same as the implications of a village conversation, which is
to say they are enormous. In a village there is if not exactly
a free and efficient marketplace of ideas, then a rough-and-
ready sorting of ideas, customs, and practices over time. Certainly a village will quickly share news of any advantageous
innovation; and if anyone gets a raise or a favorable adjustment of his rights, everyone similarly situated will soon be
pressing for the same. And why not? These people are just
like you and me, the villagers say. I can see them and hear
them every day. Why should I not have what they have?

The global conversation prompts people to ask the same
question on a global scale. In the past the educated elites
could read about democracy or capitalist prosperity. But hearing or reading of such things is not at all like having them
happen in your village, happen to people you can see and hear,
people just a few streets or broadcast frequencies away. A
global village will have global customs. In a global village, to
deny people human rights or democratic freedoms is not to
deny them an abstraction they have never experienced but
the established customs of the village. It hardly matters that
only a minority of the world's people enjoy such freedoms or
the prosperity that goes with them. Once people are convinced that these things are possible in the village, an enormous burden of proof falls on those who would deny them.

Though the global conversation generally advances both
the world economy and civil and democratic rights, all will
not participate equally. Vast regions of the earth, mostly
within the Third World, have been cut off from the information economy not only by political repression but also by
lack of the cultural and political infrastructure of a modern

society. Building these skills and structures is no easy task, but no more so than the transformation from an agrarian to an industrial society.

No one has to tell the people in favelas of Latin America or the huts of Africa that their authoritarian "command and control" economies have failed to give them even the hope of escaping from grinding poverty. The TV antennas that sprout from even the poorest settlement capture images from the global network of another way of life, one that promises to mitigate but not eliminate disparities of wealth and power. These people are ill equipped to participate in the miraculously powerful engine of wealth creation that is the information economy. Those who are without the education to participate in the knowledge society are not limited to the Third World. In the United States only one-fourth of the work force under forty have finished college, with another quarter having technical training. The half of the population that is not equipped to join the information society can nevertheless find jobs produced by that economy. Peter Drucker has pointed out:

> There is thus a real need to make non-knowledge jobs, many often requiring little skill, as productive and as self-respecting as possible. What is needed, above all, is to apply knowledge to such jobs as cleaning floors, making beds, or helping old, incapacitated people take care of themselves.[14]

The information economy thus poses social and economic problems for both the developed and developing nations at least equal to those faced in the last century.

CHAPTER FOUR

THE INFORMATION STANDARD

> How can it be that institutions that serve the
> common welfare and are extremely significant for
> its development come into being without a
> *common will* directed toward establishing them?
>
> CARL MENGER

O NE OF THE OLDEST ACTIVITIES ON THIS EARTH IS THE
trade or barter of goods and services that one person owns
for the goods or services that someone else produces. The
voluntary exchange of goods and services, which benefits
both parties, is the basis of profit and of wealth, of the easing
of want and pain. All societies engage in this exchange on
some level. Societies that arrange this exchange of value most
efficiently, easing the costs of transactions and simplifying
the long-term storage of value, have prospered more than
those that impede such exchange.

In ancient times, as the known world became larger and
more complicated, people searched for ways to settle accounts
with something of value other than the goods involved. The
invention of money, in all of its various forms, gave a huge
impetus to the volume of trade and for the first time made
capital portable. No one knows when money was first used
as a store of value and a unit of account, although the Code
of Hammurabi, written some seventeen hundred years before
Christ was born, mentions that silver was used for these pur-

55

poses. Before then, a man's wealth was expressed by the amount of land or livestock he owned, and you literally couldn't move the farm.

The transforming power of money and the markets through which it is saved, borrowed, bought, and exchanged for other currencies can hardly be exaggerated. Money and money markets create commerce and enhance the means of production by allowing action at a distance not only of space but time. They replace the accidental order of geography with an increasingly rational network of specialized efforts, varied resources, and synergistic interests. Of course, the control of such powerful tools has always seemed essential to a sovereign. From the earliest times, governments have wished to monopolize this powerful medium and mandate its value in the markets in which it is traded. The control of currency has always given a government great leverage over the most crucial material endeavors of its citizens. The regulation of money markets is the regulation of a society's resources in their most convenient and fungible form.

A traditionial aspect of sovereignty has been the power to issue currency and to control its value. In Sparta the government forbade citizens any medium of exchange other than heavy bars of iron of relatively little worth. The sons of Lycurgus correctly surmised that with such an inconvenient currency, complex commerce would be nearly impossible. The citizenry, free from the temptations of commerce, would stick to the manly art of war.

The more usual temptation, however, has been for governments to make the currency lighter, not heavier. Clipping coins so as to make them worth less than face value is an ancient tradition. And when governments learned the wonders that could be worked by printing money, a whole new era opened up. Since paper money has no intrinsic value, only scarcity value, it was both easier (or so it seemed) and more imperative for governments to control its value.

China was the first nation to issue paper currency, in the

eleventh century, but soon had to abandon the practice, as its currency was nowhere acceptable. Since that time, almost every sovereign in the world has experimented with fiat money, very often with disastrous effects. And despite a record of the continually eroding value of all the world's currency, the right to issue and control the value of money is one of the most cherished sovereign rights and onerous political duties.

The Nobel laureate F. A. Hayek has pointed out that

> . . . government's exclusive right to issue and regulate money has certainly not helped to give us a better money than we would otherwise have had, and probably a very much worse one, it has of course become a chief instrument for prevailing governmental policies and profoundly assisted the general growth of governmental power. Much of contemporary politics is based on the assumption that government has the power to create and make people accept any amount of additional money it wishes. Governments will for this reason strongly defend their traditional rights.[1]

Until recently, what we call money, whether a piece of paper, a bookkeeping entry, or a physical object, had been linked to a physical commodity that put some limit on the sovereign's ability to inflate the currency. The nature of that commodity has varied with the interests of the people using it. The early American colonists used tobacco money; the American Indians favored the cowrie shells, or wampum; and of course the more familiar copper, silver, and gold in the form of coins circulated in many parts of the world. The link between commodities and money became slowly attenuated over a long period of time. On March 6, 1933, a decisive event occurred that put the world on the road to fiat money. President Franklin D. Roosevelt issued a proclamation prohibiting American citizens from holding gold. The link was further severed on June 5, 1933, when, by a joint resolution of the U.S. Congress, the gold clause was repudiated in all private and government contracts. While various other acts were taken to weaken the tie to gold, the final blow was administered on August 15, 1971, when President Richard Nixon terminated the convertibility of the dollar into gold and the era of floating exchange rates began. Two years later, the International Monetary Fund (IMF) recognized reality and endorsed floating exchange rates. The world since that time has been operating with a monetary system for which there is no historical precedent in that no major currency in the world is currently tied to a physical commodity. The old discipline of physical commodities has now been replaced by a new kind of commodity: information.

In today's world, the value of our currency is determined by the price that the market will pay for an American dollar in exchange for yen, marks, or pounds. Whatever the price, it is almost constantly being condemned by someone somewhere as too high and by someone somewhere else as too low. Few governments are entirely satisfied with the value the market places on their currency. Someone is always demanding that government do something to push the value of its currency up or down, depending on how one's interests are affected. The volume of the clamor, as is appropriate in a democracy, is in direct proportion to the economic pain being inflicted. It is in the nature of politics to find a villain on whom to pin the blame.

Bankers are often selected for the role of scapegoat. I have been summoned by one Congress to explain why the big banks drove down the value of the dollar—described at the time as unpatriotic—and have lived long enough to be summoned by another Congress to explain why the banks keep the dollar so high that American manufacturers cannot compete abroad. In today's world, bankers are unable to do either.

There are limits to all power. The power to control the price others will pay in their currency to obtain dollars was never an exception to this rule. But today the limits on that power are more visible than ever before. Sovereign control over the value and trade of money has been irrevocably compromised and continues, gradually, to erode. That is not to say that governments can no longer influence, for better or for worse, the value of their currencies. They can and do, but their ability to readily manipulate that value in world markets is declining. Increasingly, currency values will be experienced less as a power and privilege of sovereignty than as a discipline on the economic policies of imprudent sovereigns.

This new discipline is being administered by a completely new system of international finance. Unlike all prior arrangements, this new system was not built by politicians, economists, central bankers, or finance ministers. No high-level international conference produced a master plan. The new system was built by technology.

The new world financial system is partly the accidental by-product of communication satellites and engineers learning how to use the electromagnetic spectrum up to 300 gigahertz. Just as Edison failed to foresee that his phonograph would have any commercial value, the men and women who tied the world together with telecommunications did not fully realize they were building the infrastructure of a global marketplace. Yet the money traders of the world understood immediately and drove their trades over the new global infrastructure.

The convergence of computers and telecommunications has created a new international monetary system and even a monetary standard by which the value of currencies is determined not by the arcane manipulations of central banks, whose total reserves are now dwarfed by a single day's trading on the world currency markets, but by myriad facts that are now instantaneously available.

We sit at home and watch a live broadcast of riots in a country on the other side of the earth, and a currency falls, in minutes. We hear by satellite that a leadership crisis has been resolved, and a currency rises. Ten minutes after the news of the disaster at Chernobyl was received, market data showed that stocks of agricultural companies began to move up in all world markets. For the first time in history, countless investors, merchants, and ordinary citizens can know almost instantly of breaking events all over the earth. And depending on how they interpret these events, their desire to hold more or less of a given currency will be inescapably translated into a rise or fall in its exchange value.

The natural first response to this claim is, "It has ever been so." The pressure of events has always been a major factor in determining the value of currencies. But the speed and volume of this new global market make it something different in kind and not just in degree. Cherished political, regulatory, and economic levers routinely used by sovereigns in the past are losing some of their power because the new Information Standard is not subject to effective political tinkering. It used to be that political and economic follies played to a local audience and their results could be in part contained. This is no longer true; the global market makes and publishes judgments about each currency in the world every minute and every hour of the day. The forces are so powerful that government intervention can result only in expensive failure over time.

It was not always so. After World War II, the foreign exchange market in New York was conducted by a handful of traders in the big banks, a few exchange brokers, and a rudimentary telephone system. The telex was the principle means of communications overseas where trading rooms were beginning to reopen. The volume in the currency market in the late 1940s and 1950s in New York probably did not exceed $750 million a day.

The volume of trading was small partly because complex foreign exchange controls existed in most countries in the aftermath of the war. It is the nature of government never to give up controls once established, so the controls were relaxed very slowly in most cases. One finance minister in Europe understood the stultifying nature of controls and started the train of events that has led to the present free market. Acting on a Sunday afternoon in 1948, Ludwig Erhard of Germany abolished price controls and set the German mark free. He acted on a Sunday because the occupation offices of the United States, the United Kingdom, and France were closed and so were unable to countermand the order. This action was the first of a long chain of events to abolish foreign exchange controls that made the present huge market possible.

Under the old Bretton Woods agreements a relatively small club of bankers and politicians believed it could significantly control the value of a given currency. That illusion can no longer be sustained.

When the volume of trading in anything is small, prices can be influenced dramatically by placing relatively large buy or sell orders. As the size of the market grows, the amount of orders that have to be placed to move the price either up or down becomes correspondingly larger. In the relatively small postwar money markets, central banks had enough resources to place orders large enough to influence the price of a currency. Today, with almost $2 trillion changing hands in New York alone, there is not enough money in the reserves of the world's central banks to significantly influence exchange rates on more than a momentary basis.

The new world financial market is not a geographic location to be found on a map but, rather, more than two hundred thousand electronic monitors in trading rooms all over the world that are linked together. With the new technology no one is in control. Rather, everyone is in control through collective valuations.

Technology has made us a "global" community in the literal sense of the word. Whether we are ready or not, mankind now has a completely integrated, international financial and information marketplace capable of moving money and ideas to any place on this planet in minutes. Capital will go where it is wanted and stay where it is well treated. It will flee from manipulation or onerous regulation of its value or use, and no government power can restrain it for long.

The Eurocurrency markets are a perfect example. No one designed them, no one authorized them, and no one controls them. They were fathered by interest-rate controls, raised by technology, and today they are refugees, if you will, from national attempts to allocate credit and capital for reasons that have little or nothing to do with finance and economics. Though they got their start some years before the global telecom network became the essential medium of a global financial market, their power, size, and independence were greatly augmented by that network. The two in fact matured together, demonstrating along the way that information technology makes money far more difficult to regulate than ever before.

It was in the late 1950s, roughly 1957, that the world noticed that a new money market, dominated in dollars, had begun to grow in Europe. As this market was burgeoning, government and private experts were devising schemes to improve international liquidity through various government devices. As late as 1961, Dr. Edward M. Bernstein testified before a subcommittee of the Joint Economic Committee of Congress that "while international monetary reserves are adequate at this time, it is unlikely that the growth of reserves in the future will match the greater needs of the world economy."[2] Other experts, ranging from David Rockefeller to A. Maxwell Stamp, joined in expressing concern about future world liquidity. While these experts were testifying in Congress about the coming liquidity squeeze, the greatest marshaler of liquidity in history was up and functioning. It is a strange anomaly of history that the Eurodollar market was virtually overlooked at the time.

One of the first studies of the Eurodollar market was made by Norris O. Johnson, an economist with First National City Bank (now Citibank), in about 1964. He told how irritating this new market was to some European financial experts who were accustomed to more traditional national markets. "Annoyed by imprecise usages of an undefined term, a distinguished European banker two years ago expressed the wish that he would not have to hear the word Eurodollar 'any more, anywhere, and in any sense whatsoever.' He quoted a passage from Goethe: 'Where clear notions are lacking, a word is readily invented.' " Mr. Johnson went on to say: "The banker's wish has not been fulfilled. To paraphrase Goethe: Where clear needs are present, a practice is readily invented." The study concluded as follows: "The important thing to remember about the Euromarkets is that these developments are responses to urgent economic needs. Maybe the word Eurodollar was an inappropriate coinage. But, by any name, the money is needed."[3]

How did this all come about? What were the "urgent economic needs"? In many respects the Euromarket is a monument to U.S. bank regulation. In the 1930s, the U.S. Congress, acting on the mistaken belief that high short-term interest rates were partly responsible for the 1929 crash and the ensuing depression, put legal ceilings on the rate of interest banks could pay to consumers and stopped altogether the payment of interest by banks on deposits made by corporations. So long as interest rates remained low, corporation treasurers and consumers were more or less content to accept the system. But as interest rates began to rise, individuals and corporations looked around for a way to earn an acceptable return on idle balances.

European countries fortunately did not adopt this form of price control. On the other side of the Atlantic, markets for interest rates were generally much freer, and since capital seeks the best blend of safety and return, money, including dollars, moved to Europe. Some of this money came from behind the Iron Curtain. In the mid-1950s the cold war made Communist governments nervous about depositing their dollar reserves directly in banks in the United States for fear their funds would be seized by the U.S. government. To reduce the perceived political risk, the Russians deposited their dollars in London, mostly with British banks and with Russian-controlled banks operating in Europe.

Soon the Soviets, in good non-Communist fashion, began to shop around for a higher yield on their funds. Their search took them to Italy, where it was generally believed that a banking cartel operated. Perceiving the opportunity to capitalize on this, the Soviets went to the Italian banks with an offer to place money with them if they received an interest rate higher than America's domestic law would permit but lower than the Italian banks were forced to pay for local deposits. It was a situation in which both the creditor and the borrower won. By initiating these transactions, the Soviets were in fact among the fathers of the Euromarket.

The market got a major boost in 1957 when the British government imposed controls on sterling credit in an effort to support the pound but imposed no such restrictions on dollar or European currency transactions. A futile bout with capital controls in the United States starting in 1963 gave fresh impetus to the Euromarket. As this huge market, denominated in dollars, grew in London, Mr. Paul Volcker, then under secretary of the Treasury, went to London to argue for the imposition of reserve requirements on Eurodollar deposits, as this was clearly an unregulated market. He was politely but firmly turned down. The British knew a good thing when they saw it.

During this period the famous German banker Hermann Abs was of the opinion that the Euromarket was a temporary phenomenon and would soon go away. He kept the Deutsche Bank out of the market. In the face of such a judgment, Citibank formed a task force of four or five people to report on whether the emerging Euromarket was a transitory phenomenon or a permanent source of capital. The task force's study convinced Citibank management that the market was real, and Citibank began to use the market through its London office to attract Eurodollars that could be advanced to its New

York office to fund its domestic loan portfolio. Thus, New York banks began routinely financing projects in America with dollars deposited in European banks.

From this small beginning has grown a market that is truly something new under the sun. It is now a vital part of the international financial structure of the world, vastly increased in size and speed by the increasing facility of electronic markets and the increasingly global character of the world commerce.

The Eurocurrency markets are part of a global financial network that moves capital to where it is needed and appreciates faster and more efficiently than ever before. But their very existence is a symbol of the growing futility of government attempts to regulate capital. These markets grew, as we have seen, out of a failed attempt to control capital in ways it can no longer be controlled.

It used to be that the main function of currency trading was to facilitate international trade in goods. But today the ownership of capital denominated in dollars is so huge and turning over at such speed that it totally overwhelms the money used to pay for world movements of trade. Capital transactions are now probably forty or fifty times larger than trade flows. Since this is so, the old measures of currency value that we still use, which were based on trade flows, no longer have the same meaning they once had. To further complicate matters, the usefulness of trade-weighted averages, which show a 20 percent or 30 percent decline in the dollar's value since early 1985, is reduced by the fact that America conducts about 20 percent of its bilateral trade with Latin America and Asian countries whose currencies are not usually included in this measure.

The postwar boom of the industrialized economies was based on the enlightened proposition that goods should be permitted to cross national boundaries with as few restrictions as possible. This concept was institutionalized in such international bodies as the General Agreement on Tariffs and

Trade (GATT) as well as in many national groupings. But now the global financial market extends the same freedom to money and to information about money without the benefit of government intervention.

There are, however, those who do not find this an altogether desirable development and complain that the very efficiency of the system undermines or complicates national monetary policy in particular countries. Behind that argument lies a complaint by some governments that the existence of a truly free market disciplines them when they engage in overexpansionary policies.

They are right, of course, to complain. Not only are governments losing control over money, but this newly free money in its own way is asserting its control over them, disciplining irresponsible policies and taking away free lunches everywhere. The old discipline of the gold standard has been replaced, in fact, by the new discipline of the Information Standard, more swift and more draconian than the old.

The Bretton Woods arrangement of 1944 sought to maintain fixed exchange rates, and although the conventional wisdom remembers history this way, there were, in fact, literally hundreds of currency revaluations during that period. When countries attempted to maintain an unrealistic rate, they had to use their dollar or gold reserves to buy their own currency to prop up the rate. This action almost always failed, and the country wound up with depleted reserves and an unwelcome exchange rate. The loss of reserves was one of the biggest incentives governments had to announce more realistic exchange rates. Though countries often sought to insulate themselves from the judgment of the market by instituting exchange controls, these controls always failed. Economic fundamentals always reassert themselves over time, more so now, in the new electronic marketplace for money, than ever before.

In the seventeenth century the Amsterdam bankers made

themselves unpopular in the royal chambers by weighing coins and announcing their true metallic value. Instead of weighing coins and publishing their intrinsic worth, the global market weighs the fiscal and monetary policies of each government that issues currency and places a value on it that is instantly seen by traders in Hong Kong, London, Zurich, and New York. Even major countries that announce inadequate monetary or fiscal policies have seen their foreign exchange reserves vanish in days. There is no longer enough money in the central banks of the world to hold an unrealistic exchange rate in the face of bad economic policies. Minutes after any official announcement, the Reuters screens light up in the trading rooms of the world. Scores of traders make their judgments about the effects of the new policies on the value of a currency, and then they buy or sell. These buy and sell orders drive the price up or down in minutes. The entire process does not take much more time than it took the Dutch bankers to adjust their scales in Amsterdam.

In the international financial markets today, a vote on the soundness of each country's fiscal and monetary policies, in comparison with those of every other country in the world, is held in the trading rooms of the world every minute of every day. Every kind of information moves across the electronic infrastructure that binds the world together. The latest political joke makes its way from trading room to trading room around the world in minutes. The newest figures on the GNP (gross national product), the money supply, or the words of a political leader all enter the data bases that move markets. This continuing direct plebiscite on the value of currencies and commodities proceeds by methods that are growing more sophisticated every day.

In America, we have progressed to the point where politicians no longer blame the electorate if they lose an election. Blaming the global market for our political or economic mistakes as reflected in the value of the dollar is equally useless, although some economists and politicians still do. Just as politicians often manage to trick the electorate for a short period but in the end are found out and removed from office, so central bankers, finance ministers, and parliaments sometimes imagine that their words can affect the price for currencies. But over time the market will not be fooled: Fundamentals will always prevail. The politically astute officials are the ones who see where fundamentals are driving the market and then jawbone it in that direction; hence, the phenomenon of cockcrow followed by sunrise. The best example of this was the "action" taken by a meeting of finance ministers held in the Plaza Hotel on September 22, 1985. The dollar, they opined, was overvalued. In order to rectify the situation, the ministers announced they had agreed on a course of action. The reality was that since everyone knew the dollar was overvalued, the ministers were only getting out of the way of a huge avalanche of selling that followed the announcement.

This new international monetary system is burdened with a vocabulary that was not designed to describe the modern world. The words we use do not really tell us what is happening, and so confusion abounds. It is not unlike trying to explain modern computer systems by using terms invented for describing how a steam engine works.

In the case of computers, a whole new language was invented to describe both the hardware and software; unfortunately, no such vocabulary has been developed to help us understand the new international financial system. The vocabulary we use to describe the international marketplace is largely derived from a time when merchandise trade dominated our thinking.

We talk, for example, of capital inflows or outflows, just as if money really entered our country in the way goods are unloaded from a ship. This is not the case with so-called capital inflows—no one brings dollars into America, or takes them out, for that matter. There is no capital inflow or outflow in a merchandise trade sense.

What happens is quite different. The ownership of dollars, which are already here, changes hands. If a German wants to own some dollars, he or she must buy them from someone who owns them and is willing to part with them in exchange for German marks. If the owner who sells the dollars resides in America and the buyer resides in Germany, we count the transaction as a capital inflow even though the total supply of dollars in the United States is unchanged and indeed cannot be changed except by the Federal Reserve.

All the dollars in the world—except currency—are on deposit in a bank in America, because that is the only place anyone can spend a dollar. One can, of course, give a shopkeeper abroad a dollar check in payment of merchandise, but that check will be exchanged for an equivalent amount of the local currency in which business is conducted in that country. The foreign bank that bought the dollar check for local currency will send it to New York for collection and credit to its account. Eurodollars, which are dollars deposited with a bank in London (which in turn deposits them in a bank in New York), are traded in London hundreds of times a day in huge volumes, but each transaction is effected and recorded on the books of a New York bank. After all the Eurodollar transactions have cleared, the ownership of the dollars has changed. But the number of dollars on deposit in New York remains the same in aggregate, as each debit is offset by a credit. The dollars cannot leave the system; it is a closed shop.

Doomsayers love to conjure up the specter of foreigners "pulling their dollars out of America." But we all learned in the OPEC (Organization of Oil Exporting Countries) oil crisis that, except for small amounts of currency, dollars cannot be taken out of the United States. Only the ownership of existing dollars in a bank located in America changes hands. The threat that the Arabs, the Japanese, or others would pull their dollars out of America was always an empty one, and the Arabs were well aware that it was impossible.

Even though Americans have accepted the ballot box as the arbiter of who holds office, this new global vote on the nation's fiscal and monetary policies is profoundly disturbing to many. Accepting the judgment of thousands of traders who translate politicians' actions into new values for currencies is harder to accept because it developed so fast and is new and unfamiliar. Nevertheless, it is about as useful to cuss out the thermometer for recording a heat wave as it is to rail against the values the global market puts on a nation's currency. There is no escaping the system.

In the past, nations that did not like the gold standard, the gold exchange standard, the Bretton Woods system, or whatever the dominant international financial system of the day could opt out. A finance minister would call a press conference and explain that the current international arrangements were unsatisfactory and that his nation would no longer play by the rules. This, as we have seen, is just how the gold exchange standard and later the Bretton Woods standard were dissolved.

Today there is no way for any nation to opt out of the Information Standard. No matter what formal decisions a government makes, the two hundred thousand screens in the trading rooms will continue to light up, the news will continue to march across the tube, the traders will continue to make judgments, and other traders all over the world will know instantly what value the market has placed on a currency.

Japan, which engineered a remarkable economic recovery after the war, was lauded for the skill of its policymakers in controlling markets in difficult times. As the market became freer and truly global, Japan, too, became subject to the Information Standard. In March 1990, the *New York Times* reported the erosion of sovereign power:

> Hard earned over forty years, Japan's reputation has been a source of immense confidence here, even arrogance.

But in the last three months, that reputation has begun to unravel. For the first time, market forces are looming larger than the powers of Government bureaucrats.

Persistent turmoil has racked the financial markets this year, sending stock prices down by more than 20 percent, the yen down more than 5 percent and interest rates up sharply, despite numerous Government attempts to restore order. As a result, Japan's elite bureaucrats are watching their credibility erode almost daily.[4]

The rapid dissemination of information has always changed societies and their governments. In the case of the Information Standard, governments have lost even more than the power to freely manipulate their currencies or the ability to protect their currencies from their own economic folly. The new system also is steadily driving sovereign nations toward unprecedented international cooperation and coordination of monetary and fiscal policies.

The slow building and knitting together of the European Economic Community (EEC) is a case in point. Today we have a kind of mini–Bretton Woods agreement among the countries in the community called the European Monetary System, or EMS. It is not a fixed-rate system, as there has been a realignment of currencies each year, but it is anchored by the German deutsche mark, just as the old system was based on the dollar. The system itself forces all participating governments to weigh heavily the actions of their neighbors in forming their own policy. It is almost the reverse of the old mercantilism. Money is only one of the problems of living in an integrated world. The vast bureaucracy in Brussels is trying to "harmonize" everything from the kind of plug to use on an electric razor to what frequencies can be used in satellite transmission. All of these efforts and thousands more are being forced by integration of the market. Each nation will always pursue what it perceives to be its own national interest, but it cannot do so in a vacuum. If one government in the market approves a new drug to alleviate suffering and another does not because of official doubts about it, citizens will cross borders to be treated. This is but one example of many thousands of events that will occur and indeed are now happening that will move governments toward adopting common standards.

The global network has become such an essential part of the future of the world that it is worthy of everyone's best efforts to see that it remains as efficient, as cost-effective, and as free as possible.

The legitimate competing concerns of society make this no easy task, but it is one that is worthy of our best efforts because the global marketplace has become such an essential part of the future of the world. The ability to move capital to where it is needed and wanted is fundamental to the continuous effort of mankind to live a better life. In today's world, information about this market and the transfers themselves travel on our networks at the speed of light—which Einstein tells us is as fast as it is possible to go. Keeping that data moving with speed and efficiency while balancing competing interests is our particular challenge—and the greatest contribution we can make to the world that emerges from the information explosion.

As the relative weight of the world economy outside any given sovereign state increases, the need for international cooperation also increases. In June 1989, Federal Reserve chairman Alan Greenspan called on other central bankers to cooperate in overseeing international markets. He urged central bankers to work together to supervise multinational payment and clearing systems rather than create a centralized authority. The growing practice of "netting" debits and credits in each country is leading, Mr. Greenspan said, to the "decentralization of the major monetary mechanisms" and could diminish the supervisory power of central banks. No leader likes to face the erosion of his or her own power. Central bankers are no different in that regard than others, but the world has changed, and central bankers, acting alone in their own country, no longer can control financial events in the way they once could. The huge capital movements that wash across the world, the international arbitrage of interest rates, the global futures market, and above all, the communications ability that permits individuals to move their money away from danger and toward a safe haven rob individual central banks of much of their power. The views of the chairman of the Federal Reserve Board are among the first to highlight this new situation, but they will not be the last to decry the erosion of sovereign power. Indeed, the process has just begun.

The END OF THE TRADE

No nation was ever ruined by trade.
BENJAMIN FRANKLIN

THROUGHOUT HISTORY A DISPUTE HAS RAGED ABOUT THE way to achieve economic progress. Thucydides, the great historian of the Peloponnesian Wars, understood clearly the role of trade in the fifth century B.C.:

> Without commerce, without freedom of communication either by land or sea, cultivating no more of their territory than the exigencies of life required, (people) could never rise above nomadic life and consequently neither built large cities nor attended to any other form of greatness.

But the concept that trade produces human progress and the lack of it condemns people to mere subsistence has not been universally shared. This ancient animosity toward trade and commerce as a way to increase the wealth of nations dies hard, and until the eighteenth century the free flow of trade was seldom seen as advantageous.

The maps we look at today and the trading relationships that we now take for granted bear little resemblance to those we knew a generation ago. For example, what we now know as Germany consisted only two hundred years ago of over a thousand economic units separated by customs barriers and guild regulations. While the Germans were still living in commercial isolation from one another, the United Kingdom had long been a common market. Martin Wolf has written:

> This difference was one of the main reasons why the Industrial Revolution started here, the significance of the internal barriers being shown by the great rapidity with which the German economy caught up, once a custom union (the Zollverein) had been put in place during the nineteenth century.[1]

The United States enjoyed a similar advantage. Shortly after Chief Justice Burger retired, I asked him what he regarded as the most important sections of the U.S. Constitution, and he answered immediately, "The First Amendment and the commerce clause." The latter, he explained, made possible our continental common market, which created the circumstances for America's economic growth.

For hundreds of years the world has been torn between the extremes of economic nationalism and the concept of worldwide free trade, a debate that raises the most serious questions concerning the state's power and wealth, to say nothing of its fundamental purpose. The case for free markets, according to F. A. Hayek, is that

> the market is the only known method of providing information enabling individuals to judge comparative advantages of different uses of resources of which they have no immediate knowledge and through whose use, whether they so intend or not, they serve the needs of distant unknown individuals. This dispersed knowledge is *essentially* dispersed, and cannot possibly be gathered together and conveyed to an authority charged with the task of deliberately creating order.[2]

The mercantile system of the sixteenth, seventeenth, and eighteenth centuries, on the contrary, was a political endeavor to maintain and extend the power of government not only abroad but at home by attempting to regulate all kinds of production—a concept that bordered on absurdity when Jean-Baptiste Colbert, Louis XIV's controller general, decreed even the size of a handkerchief and the length of a fish that could come to market. According to Colbert: "All purchases must be made in France, rather than in foreign countries, even if the goods should be a little poorer and a little more expensive, because if the money does not go out to the realm, the advantage to the state is double." Although mercantilism, like most political concepts, was variously expressed by many people, the central point of mercantilism was a belief that "the greatness of a state is measured entirely by the quantity of silver it possesses."[3] The purpose of the state, in other words, was primarily to enrich the royal treasury, not to enhance commerce or encourage the division of labor.

To further this goal, the object of the mercantilistic game was to export goods abroad and import precious metals in payment. The gold and silver thus acquired, so the argument ran, paid for the armies and navies that fought and won the wars that increased the territory and power of the state. Soldiers and sailors at that time put little faith in the promises of kings and demanded gold in payment for their services and later only reluctantly accepted silver. So gold was necessary to maintain an army, and selling goods abroad for bullion was one way to produce it.

In 1776, Adam Smith, as we have seen, challenged the principles of the mercantilistic system, arguing for freer trade and the concept of laissez-faire. Smith further argued that the wealth of a country was directly connected to "the increase of the number of its inhabitants" rather than the size of its gold reserve. Smith saw that the size of the market was central to his concept of the division of labor, although in his wildest dreams he could never have contemplated today's global market. As usual, he put it succinctly: "As it is the power of exchanging that gives occasion to the division of labor, so the extent of this division must always be limited by the extent of that power or, in other words, by the extent of the market."[4]

The power of sovereign states to control commerce between its citizens and the citizens of other nations has been a jealously guarded right as long as nation-states have existed. From before the time of Adam Smith, national governments understood that to control a nation's economy, to advance one particular goal or frustrate that one, to help this group at the expense of another, to reward friends and punish enemies, states must control international trade. They must, that is, assert the power of the state over that of their citizens to decide which deals get done, which foreign companies are tolerated, and which national companies are promoted.

Today this traditional sovereign power is eroding almost as rapidly as the power of individual states to control the short-term fluctuations in the value of their own currencies. It is eroding largely because the classic concept of international trade is becoming obsolete. The traditional multinational economy in which "products" are exported is being replaced by a truly global one in which value is added in several countries. The traditional business of import and export among nations is being replaced by a transnational system of product development, design, production, and marketing that takes less and less notice of national borders and which national governments can disrupt only at the risk of economic chaos far greater than the protectionist disasters of the past. The world has been moving, fitfully and with many reversals, toward a global economy almost from the beginning of time. But this process has accelerated enormously in the past few dcades largely because the growing global information network, global financial markets, and improvements in transportation have greatly eased the difficulties of international trade and production. This information infrastructure has also encouraged consumers and businesses worldwide to demand the same sorts of products at the best prices and quality, requirements that can be met only by access to a global market. We have not yet arrived at the point where government policy has shifted from protecting its natural-resources base from foreign capital and has moved toward policies that assure their citizens access to the best products at the lowest prices. But consumers are already demanding such a shift in many countries of the world because they are learning more and more about the world's goods as displayed on television.

This acceleration toward a global economy has produced a fundamental change in the world's work. The driving force behind that change is information technology and in particular the relative importance of intellectual capital in relation to physical capital. Intellectual capital—human intelligence—is now the dominant factor of production, and the world's most fundamentally important market is the market for intellectual capital. The most mobile of all forms of capital will be increasingly intolerant of nationalist restrictions because it is inherently global and almost immune from nationalist restrictions. Far more than any other form of capital, intellectual capital will go where it is wanted, stay where it is well treated, and multiply where it is allowed to earn the greatest return. Nations that respect the freedom of intellectual capital and accommodate it accordingly will prosper in the global economy. Those that imagine that this most powerful form of capital can be enslaved or entailed will wither.

For roughly the entire history of the industrial era annual growth in international trade has outstripped yearly GNP (gross national product) growth for the advanced economies, the only exception being the years between 1914 and 1950, when two world wars and an outbreak of protectionism interrupted the peaceful growth of world prosperity.[5] In the past three decades, however, world trade has grown particularly rapidly despite a recent slowdown in the world economy and occasional outbreaks of protectionism—mostly in the form of nontariff barriers, such as national buying policies and import quotas.[6]

From 1950 to 1985, while real-world GNP tripled, world trade grew sevenfold. America's merchandise exports more than doubled in the decade ending in 1987, from $120,816 million to $249,570 million.[7] Among the Western industrial powers the percentage of the GNP absorbed by foreign trade has almost doubled since 1960.[8] In the United States, which has the world's largest internal market, foreign trade has, until recently, represented an almost insignificant single-digit percentage of our national efforts. But by the mid-1980s, merchandise imports and exports accounted for over 15 percent of the U.S. GDP (gross domestic product). In Europe, with their far smaller internal markets, the figures were even more arresting: By 1986, merchandise trade accounted for more than 20 percent of France's GNP, more than 40 percent of Great Britain's, and almost 50 percent of West Germany's.[9] The creation of the European Economic Community (EEC) was therefore a foregone conclusion, and the complete integration of the European nations will increase these numbers even further.

Yet none of these figures count trade in services, the most rapidly growing sector of world trade. The reason for the absence of service figures is partly historical and partly practical. For years, government statisticians used the cash, insurance, and freight (CIF) method to value the goods sold in international trade, thus incorporating these services in the value of merchandise trade. Only a few years ago, the model that economists built of the world economy did not have to account for services, but now such models are unacceptable; shipping companies, airlines, travel companies, financial institutions, consulting firms, accountants, and lawyers are all engaged in this kind of service trade. The importance of trade in services was recognized on September 20, 1986, when trade ministers from all over the world, meeting in Punta del Este, Uruguay, agreed for the first time to make trade in services a major issue in GATT (General Agreement on Tariffs and Trade) negotiations. Nor do the trade numbers include the huge movement of money capital that by far exceeds world trade. Many of these transactions can be effected only by buying or selling foreign exchange, so the size of this market had to expand and is now probably about $500 billion per day and growing. While these numbers are tricky in that they may include double counting between institutions, they nevertheless indicate a market of a size, depth, and speed never before seen on earth, one that presents entirely new problems for sovereign states.

It used to be that each sovereign policed and regulated the markets operating in its own country with small regard to what was happening elsewhere. Each country now has its own clearance system by which trades are settled, each its own rules of trading, its own margin requirements and trading hours and holidays. Even though markets are now blips on a screen and not geographic locations, sovereigns still try to protect and control that part of the market that functions within its jurisdiction. Yet even this becomes increasingly difficult, for if one sovereign becomes unreasonable in the severity of regulatory demands, the market node in that country withers and is replaced by the node "residing" in more hospitable climes. To be effective, a sovereign must therefore cooperate with other governments in forging international agreements.

This problem was acknowledged officially by the Bank for International Settlements—a kind of a central bank's bank—in a study released in March 1989, which concluded that "the appropriate division and sharing of supervisory responsibilities will be extremely problematic."

While creating massive problems for government regulation, the electronic market occasionally solves problems by eliminating geography. The fierce rivalries that have split stock trading among seven regional exchanges in the tiny country of Switzerland prevented the opening of a Swiss futures and options exchange because no city would tolerate its location in any other. In the meantime, the business was going to London and Amsterdam. Saul Hansell tells us: "The solution was to redefine an exchange. The . . . Swiss Options and Financial Futures Exchange is not in Geneva nor Zurich nor any other city; trading occurs in the dimensionless geography of a computer network."[10]

The enormous explosion of world trade has not only created a global market, but the worldwide information network has made it possible to carry the division of labor through all states of production and marketing, with value added in many countries. An item in a showroom with a well-known brand name such as IBM may in fact be only a handsome facade hiding parts from all over the world. The popular IBM PS/2 Model 30-286, for example, contains a microprocessor from Malaysia, oscillators from either France or Singapore; disk controller logic array, diskette controller, ROM, and video graphics array from Japan; VLSI circuits and video digital-to-analog converter from Korea; and Dram from Singapore, Japan, or Korea—and all this is put together in Florida. To complicate matters further, some components are manufactured overseas, but by a U.S. company.[11] Since there are thousands of such products put together in similar ways, the old concept of trading one item for another is obsolete. But the bookkeeping system to record these international transactions has not changed. When measuring systems fail to keep up with technology, they become less and less useful, and through them we understand less and less about the world economy.

The current trade accounting system is totally inadequate to produce any useful numbers for policymakers concerning the following transaction: An American author exports intellectual capital in the form of a manuscript to Taiwan, where it is printed and bound into a book. The book is then shipped back to the United States to be sold in bookstores

81

here. The export of the manuscript, which from a physical standpoint is small, barely shows in tallying up U.S. exports, but the finished book at, say, two dollars per copy shows up as part of the value of Taiwan's exports. The books are sold in this country for thirty dollars by American stores, and royalties accrue to an American author. So far as the balance-of-trade figures are concerned, Taiwan runs a trade surplus with the United States, and we appear to have a trade deficit with Taiwan. Clearly this accounting does not reflect reality, since the lion's share of the return on this capital is generated in the United States. These trends toward horizontal integration are being driven by the growing awareness that to survive in the global market, everyone has to go back to basics and pursue a form of comparative advantage. In this example, Taiwan did have such an advantage in actually printing and binding books, but the United States had the advantages of creating both the intellectual capital and the marketing strategy.

As the volume of world trade increases, so does the complexity of trade patterns and the number of significant players. Long dominated by the Developed Market Economies, essentially Western Europe, the United States, and Japan, the club of major trading nations is growing quickly.

Since 1965, the developing countries' share of world manufactured exports has risen from 7.3 to more than 17 percent. Most of this increase is due to newly industrialized countries (NICs), such as Hong Kong, South Korea, Singapore, and Brazil, all of which now rank among the top twenty exporters of manufactured goods, though no developing country ranked among the top thirty as recently as 1965.[12] India, Indonesia, and others are coming on quickly. Several of these countries—Korea is a particularly strong example—have become driving forces in regional development. With growing prosperity and rising wages at home, such companies have begun to move labor-intensive manufacturing jobs to their less developed neighbors and in turn have helped those lesser developed neighbors become more important markets for NIC manufacturers.

Among the developed countries and NICs, the exchange of products has become more egalitarian, making the warp and woof of trade more complex and difficult to unravel. In the first post–World War II decades, the United States thoroughly dominated the sale of high- and mid-technology products; world trade patterns in such products resembled the spokes of a wheel of which the United States was the hub. As recently as the late 1960s, Japanese cars were regarded with amusement, and "made in Japan" (or Hong Kong) were bywords for inferiority. Today all the developed countries and most of the NICs can produce a vast number of products and components that approach state of the art. As a result, trade flows of sophisticated products move from country to country for value-added components, assembly, and packaging.

Much of this trade, particularly in information-rich technologies, is carried on within, or facilitated by, an increasingly complex network of alliances between companies sharing precious technological and intellectual resources. This sharing of intellectual capital may take the form of jointly developed products, filling in each other's product lines, supplying each other's cutting-edge components, or simply availing themselves of the best and the latest in today's blisteringly fast technological competition. With technology and manufacturing capabilities so widespread, the international sourcing of competitively priced components is no longer a luxury but a necessity from which no country's businesses can afford to be cut off. As Christopher Bartlett of the Harvard Business School has written, "Competitiveness is already beyond the reach of the purely national company."[13]

The year 1989 marked the tenth anniversary of the creation of the world's largest producer of commercial jet engines, a company that hardly anyone outside the industry has heard of. The company, CFM International, is a joint venture of SNECMA (a French government company) and GE, which is, of course, a private American company. This new entity is managed jointly by a third company called CFMI. The official press release of July 18, 1989, celebrating the anniversary, explained the workings of an enterprise that has produced two thousand jet engines, with three thousand more on order.

> CFMI has a small staff to act as project manager and as the contractual interface with customers. But CFMI does none of the engineering, manufacturing, marketing, or project support work itself. It buys that work from SNECMA and GE, balancing the work shares so that they reflect the 50/50 ownership of the program. CFMI also splits the sales revenues between the two parents.

This complex but highly efficient structure was constructed to help fulfill the French government's desire to enlarge its role in the world market for commercial aircraft engines and GE's desire to sell two of its new aircraft engine designs to Airbus Industries, a European consortium, which was going to build a new 150-passenger airliner. The technology of the engine core, which is built by GE in Cincinnati, Ohio, is not shared with the French partners due to restrictions mandated by the U.S. government. But the French have significant technologies that are likewise hidden from the Americans. While the engine cores come from America, SNECMA builds the low-pressure outer parts of the engine in France. Some engines are assembled in GE's plant in Evendale, Ohio, and some in SNECMA's facility in Villaroche, France. The engines are sold all over the world to civilian airlines and also to power more than three hundred military aircraft in six countries.

This very successful international venture is only one example of why it is becoming more and more difficult to unscramble the egg as global manufacturing and marketing alliances are becoming the rule rather than the exception. Nevertheless, protectionism has had its effects: A good deal of trade has been transferred into foreign investment, as companies avoid quotas and other nontariff barriers by assembling or producing final products in the countries in which they mean to sell them. Thus, Honda now builds more cars in America than in Japan. Roughly half of American chemical workers work for foreign-owned companies.[14] In 1987, some thirteen hundred American and European companies made and sold over $260 billion worth of goods in Japan, accounting for 10.9 percent of Japan's GNP.[15] But this trend, not all of which is due to protectionism, only strengthens the global economy and makes it more difficult for economic nationalists to control or subvert it by substituting products made locally by foreign companies.

This expanding pattern of world trade in goods is largely a function of information technology, for not only has the global telecom network made global enterprise far more practical; products become easier and more profitable to trade as information becomes the dominant source of value added. A few ounces of microchips or a few pounds of VCRs may earn more profit than a ton of steel, though steel itself is made by an information-rich new system that today packs more strength and value per pound than it did a decade ago. The cost of actually moving high-technology products around the world is now such an insignificant percentage of their selling price that a growing percentage of such products travels air freight. So cross-border business agreements are limited not by cost so much as by the imagination of the participants. For example, one division of General Electric, Power Systems, has sixteen alliances with sixty-two companies located in nineteen countries. These types of arrangements are becoming typical of all large companies, no matter where their headquarters may be located.

The automobile business is a classic example of alliances covering everything from engineering to production. Chrysler, for example, owns 24 percent of Mitsubishi Motors, which in turn owns part of the South Korean company Hyundai. Additionally, automobiles bearing the Chrysler logo are made by Mitsubishi, and a fifty-fifty joint venture of the companies in Illinois will be producing cars under both nameplates. Ford owns 25 percent of Mazda, and Mazda makes cars in America for Ford, and Ford makes trucks for Mazda. Each one of these companies owns a piece of Korea's Kia Motors. Ford and Nissan swap vehicles in Australia, while Ford and Volkswagen are a single company in Latin America that exports trucks to the United States. General Motors owns 41 percent of Isuzu, which is starting a joint venture in America with Subaru, which in turn is partly owned by Nissan.[16] And so it goes. Europe is also full of such alliances, which grow in number and complexity every day. These ventures range from relatively arm's length relationships, such as licensing and outsourcing, to more formal "alliances," consortia, joint ventures, and mergers.

During the 1980s, high-technology firms, such as Siemens (FRG), Philips (Benelux), GGE, Bull, and Thomson (France), Olivetti (Italy), AT&T, IBM, Control Data, Fujitsu, Toshiba, and NEC (Japan), each forged numerous foreign alliances; some of them formed dozens.[17] A chart of Siemens's international cooperative agreements is a genealogist's delight, including, among others, Ericsson, Toshiba, Fujitsu, Fuji, GTE, Corning Glass, Intel, Xerox, KTM, Philips, B. E., GEC, Thomson, Microsoft, and World Logic Systems. IBM has so many alliances in Japan that there is a Japanese book on the subject called *IBM's Alliance Strategy in Japan.*

The driving force behind all these diverse combinations is the need to make the most out of increasingly precious and highly mobile intellectual capital. Research and development (intellectual capital investment) has become a huge fixed cost for many high- (and medium-) technology companies. A new drug may cost $300 million to develop; a new jet engine, a billion. Moreover, the pace of technological development means that even a highly successful R & D effort may in the end not come up with a state-of-the-art product but, rather, with an expensive also-ran.

While politicians still talk of international trade and a few industrialists echo their statements, the integration of the world's production is destroying the reason that a balance-of-merchandise trade should exist between countries. The trade deficit that was supposed to destroy America did not for the reasons we have mentioned. It can be argued that the very concept of a trade balance is an artifact from a bygone age. As long as capital—both human and money—can move freely toward opportunity, trade will not balance; indeed, one will have as little reason to desire such accounting symmetry between nations as between, say, New York State and California. We have built the beginnings of what George Gilder has called a "planetary utility."

The most remarkable example of economic integration, on a regional basis, is the rapid progress being made by the EEC toward turning Europe into a single market. There will continue to be setbacks along the way, some serious, but nevertheless remarkable progress is being made. The EEC was formally established in 1958 as an outgrowth of an earlier effort to form the European Coal and Steel Community. After languishing in the backwaters of national politics for years, the explosive growth of the world economy focused attention on the attractiveness of a huge integrated market in Europe, and a target date of 1992 was set to achieve it. By that date, the EEC nations intend to have dramatically eased the movement of people, goods, and money across national borders, harmonized thousands of national regulations and more than a hundred thousand technical standards; sweep away onerous barriers to trade and entry, and lower the costs of doing business throughout the community.

This effort is remarkable first because the single most common argument one hears for it is that European companies need guaranteed access to a much larger market than that afforded by their home countries if they are to support the development of information-rich products.

The other remarkable thing about the pursuit of the single

market is that a new generation of European business leaders has not waited for the political process to adjust to the information age but have sought to adjust it. The single market is more advanced in fact than in law, as business practice has outpaced legal reform. The armies of civil servants who stamp entry documents and compute border taxes are understandably not enthusiastic about seeing their jobs eliminated.

Clearly, a common currency will be the final step in a completely integrated market, and the EEC has moved toward this eventuality, but this surrender of sovereignty touches the very heart of the nation-state. To lose control of the right to issue currency is an attack against one of sovereignty's most valued rights. As trade between European countries grew, as business alliances proliferated, and as money capital was needed from wherever savings existed, the need arose for a unit of account that would be relatively immune from the changing relationships among national currency values. Several ideas were put forth, but most centered on some kind of a basket of currencies so that no particular devaluation or reevaluation would overwhelm the rest. After a few false starts, the European Currency Unit (ECU) emerged as the market's way to solve a problem. The ECU looks like a currency and is used like a currency, but it lacks one essential element, and that is the backing of some national or international monetary authority. The matter is further complicated by the fact that about the same time as the market was creating the ECU, governments were establishing a similar unit with the same name created by the European monetary authorities through swaps with European central banks. These institutions thus become obligated to exchange 20 percent of their gold and dollar reserves for official ECUs. These official ECUs are not convertible into any single currency and cannot be traded. Additionally, the failure to establish a European monetary fund has given these official ECUs a certain fragility that has prevented it from emerging as a reserve currency. The private ECU, on the other hand, which grew up in response to market demand, is growing in usefulness all the time. Corporations are using the ECU for denominating notes, bonds, and accounting entries. In 1989, there were 114 bond issues totaling 11.2 billion ECUs, up from 71 issues for 6.6 billion in 1987. The percentage of bonds issued in ECUs as against all bond issues stayed steady at about 4 percent. There has also been put in place an ECU clearing system that handles billions of ECUs a day and has become a vital part of the new, emerging European system. Today, more than five hundred banks lend, take deposits, and deal in the private ECU in the same way they handle any other currency. Some governments have even used the private ECU in their money-raising efforts in Europe. The Japanese government, for example, guaranteed an issue of Japanese highway bonds in 1987 denominated in ECUs. What has happened, in effect, is that the governments, by not moving quickly enough to establish a usable common currency, have been bypassed by the market, which has created its own international currency, albeit of limited utility. Although not accepted as legal tender by any European government, the ECU grows in importance every year, since more companies need a stable European unit of account for cross-border contracts and a simpler and more accurate way to report the fortunes of pan-European businesses. The official movement toward creating a common currency in the EC (European Community) was given impetus at the meeting of ministers held in Holland in late 1991, but in the meantime private ECU is serving a very useful purpose.

The single market comes at a real cost in traditional national power and sovereign prerogatives: Brussels, where the European Commission and the European Parliament are located, now entertains more lobbyists than any city in the world other than Washington, testimony to how much power has shifted toward this transsovereign body. But this shift in power, though guided by European leaders of admirable vision and leadership, came largely in response to economic and social forces, which in turn were driven by the information technology that made Europe into a de facto common market long before the national governments might have wished.

WHERE WE STAND

> A . . . useful and somewhat surprising lesson of
> historical scholarship is that widely accepted facts
> are often wrong.
>
> GEORGE STIGLER,
> *Memoirs of an Unregulated Economist*

WE ARE SO ACCUSTOMED TO THE VARIOUS STANDARDS OF measurement we commonly use that we seldom stop to consider either their validity for today's world or their history. We have a surfeit of numbers quantifying every aspect of life. This was not always the case. The historian Fernand Braudel tells us, for example: "Nobody knows the total population of the world between the fifteenth and eighteenth centuries . . . the figures are few and not very reliable. They apply only to Europe and . . . to China . . . What about the rest of the world? There is nothing in fact on non-Chinese Asia, outside Japan,"[1]

The measurements of time and distance we use today evolved slowly, and each refinement often ran into resistance from those with a vested interest in the familiar measures. Time is a good case in point. The Egyptians developed one of the first successful measuring devices when it occurred to them to use the sun's shadow to measure the passage of time. The result was the first crude sundial. With admirable, if misplaced, logic they located the hour markings equidistantly from each other. We now know that this actually produced

91

hours of uneven length, varying with the seasons of the year. But since there were no alternative measuring devices, people became accustomed to relying on these somewhat eccentric instruments and were convinced they were accurate.

About five hundred years after the first sundial was constructed, the Egyptians invented the water clock. The artisans were dismayed to discover that their new water clocks did not tell the same time as the sundials. They assumed that the sundials, which had been used for centuries, were correct and spent considerable time and treasure in frustrating attempts to construct a water clock precisely as inaccurate as a sundial. It was not until the fourteenth century that mechanical clocks were constructed that produced accurate measures of the passing hours. Town clocks in that era had no hands or dials, as the populace was illiterate, but did ring bells to mark the passing hours.[2]

When we encounter a new situation, we assess it against some yardstick of our experience. We are now in the midst of a huge technological and economic revolution. Yet we are so accustomed to using the standards of economic and social measurement developed for the industrial age that we seldom stop to consider that the old measures of economic progress and decay, success and failure, are rapidly losing their usefulness. Much of the economic hysteria that has become a constant background to discussions of government policy or business strategy is traceable to the increasing inaccuracy or irrelevance of our standards of economic measurement. The declining usefulness of these standards seems to be one reason so many very good economists lately have been so wrong about the direction of the economy. For the last seven or eight years of the decade of the 1980s, the standard blue-chip economic forecast went like this: "We are surprised how strong this quarter is, but we expect the next quarter to be weaker and the recession to occur four or five quarters out." Words like these resounded from innumerable podiums over that time period. The problem with this standard forecast was that for a very long time it was wrong, although like a stopped clock that is right twice a day, it momentarily described reality. What these failed forecasts demonstrate is that even very good people will make bad calls when they must use bad information.

Flying by faulty instruments is dangerous. The old instruments may convince us we have failed where we are succeeding or persuade us to turn about in vain pursuit of our past rather than successfully navigating the future. If we are to cope successfully with the information economy, we shall have to develop a new methodology to measure economic success and failure.

In some cases this may mean merely updating and revising measurements that have served us well for many years. But in other cases we must be prepared to give up forever the statistical surety of the old numbers in favor of less quantifiable indicators. America's balance of trade figures, which are much lamented, today conceal more than they reveal. Murray Weidenbaum has written:

> Two basic statistical indicators make the point: The first is that one-half of all imports and exports are transacted between companies and their foreign affiliates or parents. From the viewpoint of political geography, these are international transactions. But from an economic and technological viewpoint, the flow of goods and services are internal transfers within the same enterprise. A second way of looking at the global market is to consider that one-half of the products manufactured in the U. S. have one or more foreign components.[3]

(Our current accounting conventions fail to take these new realities into account.)

Knowledge, the fundamental capital stock of the information economy, is far more difficult to quantify than the material wealth and real assets that previously dominated economic thought. As it becomes clear that today really is different from yesterday, nations may be forced not only to change the way they measure their economies but also to modify their ambitions to regulate and control them. If it turns out that the economy of the future really is fundamentally more difficult to measure than the economy of the past, governments may have to relinquish many of the powers of economic planning and control they have acquired over the past several hundred years.

George Stigler, the Nobel laureate who has done such brilliant work on the consequence of economic policies, put the problem this way:

> The first and the purest demand of society is for scientific knowledge, knowledge of the consequences of economic actions. . . . Whether one is a conservative or a radical, a protectionist or a free trader, a cosmopolitan or a nationalist, a churchman or a heathen, it is useful to know the causes and consequences of economic phenomena . . . Such scientific information is value-free in the strictest sense; no matter what one seeks, he will achieve it more efficiently the better his knowledge of the relationship between action and consequences.[4]

In order to get that information, we must measure things impartially. This is easier said than done. Einstein's theory could be proved by using the photographs of a solar eclipse. The wealth of nations is more elusive. Not long ago in historical terms, land and wealth were seen to be one and the same. So were other natural resources. Then, as the Industrial Revolution remade Western society, economists only gradually accepted manufacturing as a creator of wealth.

In the 1980s, as the industrial age began to fade into the information society, the same arguments took place but with different protagonists. Making "things" in a factory, not punching computer keys, created wealth, we were told. The measurements of wealth and progress we have become accustomed to in the industrial age may be no more relevant to the information society than the *Domesday Book* of William the Conqueror, which recorded ownership of parcels of land, was central to wealth creation in the industrial age.

In modern times, one of the principal sets of measures published by our government is the National Income and Products Accounts, which yield, among other things, the official estimate of the gross national product (GNP). These statistical measures were constructed during the Great Depression when our GNP was about $56 billion, the economy was dominated by traditional heavy industry, and national exports, at $500 million, accounted for less than 1 percent of the GNP. By any reckoning measurement of the GNP is an immensely difficult task, and one can only admire the skill of the people who constructed our national accounting system. But given the dramatic changes in the economies of the United States and the world, too great a reliance on sixty-year-old national income accounts puts us in real danger of mismeasuring the economy. Since fiscal 1969, the U.S. government has used a unified cash-based budget that does not produce results congruent with generally accepted accounting principles. One of the principal aberrations from good accounting principles is that there are no capital accounts. Everything the government buys is "expensed"—a several-billion-dollar road system, Yellowstone National Park, or a ten-cent pencil. It would be hard to find a serious accountant who would endorse this bookkeeping system. Its employment in the private sector might force prosecution for fraud.

Today's method of calculating the GNP not only fails—except indirectly—to capture the benefits of rapidly accumulating knowledge, but it is also marred by inconsistencies. For example, income is imputed by formula to the owners of homes that they occupy, but there are no imputations for streams of income that flow from the use of autos, dishwashers, and other consumer durables. In times of high taxation, these durables—which are arguably capital investments—often provide shelter from the ravages of inflation. Because of these and other difficulties it becomes increasingly arduous to measure recent GNP achievements and much more formidable to make projections into the future.

Government is incapable even of telling us with any precision what the last quarter's GNP growth was. Final figures are not issued until three years after the close of a quarter. The difference between the Commerce Department's first reports on the GNP for a quarter and the final figures show huge variations. If, for example, the initial report indicated a GNP growth of 3 percent, virtually a full 50 percent of the time the final figures show statistical growth of either less than 1.5 percent or more than 4.5 percent. One time in ten the adjusted final figure would be recorded as less than 0.5 percent of more than 5.5 percent. Figures that vary that much rarely furnish a firm foundation for policy decisions. The record of looking ahead for most forecasters, public or private, is even worse.

Yet the GNP and other national economic measurements play a critical role in the formulation of economic policy. The federal deficit is a case in point. Federal fiscal policy depends on accurate forecasts of the deficit, which in turn depend very heavily on GNP projections. Yet the numbers produced by the Congressional Budget Office (CBO) are often substantially at variance with those produced by the Office of Management and Budget (OMB), an agency of the executive branch. For the fiscal year 1991, the CBO estimated the federal deficit at $138 billion, while the OMB projected a deficit of $63.1 billion— a difference of $74.9 billion. Political agendas obviously intrude on these supposedly objective measurements. Doom and gloom clashes with a rosy scenario, and it becomes ever more difficult to tell who is right.

Federal Reserve monetary policy is heavily dependent on comparing GNP estimates with estimates of the nation's productive capacity. What rightly concerns Fed policymakers is how fast the real economy can grow over the long haul without inflation. What is the real potential growth rate for real GNP? The Fed, as nearly as one can infer from its public statements, assumes the GNP has the potential to grow at around 3 percent before running into the physical limitations imposed by capacity. The Fed may act to slow growth if the economy grows at the persistently higher rate in order to slow inflation. On the other hand, some of the Fed's supply-side critics insist that potential GNP growth is as high as 5 percent. The issue is anything but trivial. The difference between a 3 and 5 percent potential could mean a huge difference in the level of real GNP over a ten-year span. Clearly reliable assessments of potential growth are essential, and deciding the reliability of these measures in turn rests in part on whether or not current measures of industrial capacity remain relevant in the information age.

Some argue that when industrial production reaches approximately 85 percent of capacity, the economy approaches the physical limits of its output, raising the possibility that further growth will be inflationary. In today's economy this traditional rule of thumb may be outmoded, since industrial production employs only about 20 percent of American labor, with the balance working in the nonindustrial sectors of our society, where there remains a huge potential for expansion.

Despite the decline in the percentage of nonfarm workers employed in manufacturing—from 31 percent to 19 percent today—manufacturing as a share of the GNP has remained remarkably stable throughout the postwar period. We have seen in our factories the same phenomenon that so dramatically changed American farms. Fewer and fewer people are producing more and more goods. It is estimated that in 1810, 80 percent of the labor force was employed in agriculture; by 1910 it had fallen to about 30 percent; and today it is roughly 3 percent—and yet we can and do feed the world.[5]

This relatively steady output, in the face of a massive exodus of workers from industry, raises the question of whether the utilization figures on percentage of industrial capacity mean the same thing for inflation as they once did. Indeed, this measure of capacity utilization played a key role in leading some forecasters to overestimate inflation during the 1982–87 economic expansion. Another reason the capacity utilization index misleads unwary economists is that it covers only manufacturing, mining, and utilities, activities that account for a shrinking share of U.S. output.

The standard industrial codes that once told how industry is organized are now out-of-date. Of the twelve major code divisions, only two reflect the service industry, although about 80 percent of Americans work in a service business. Accurate numbers are available on the number of brakemen on American railroads but not on the number of computer programmers. This is but one example of why today's economy cannot be fitted into yesterday's standards. If basic macroeconomic measurements, such as the GNP and productive capacity, do not mean what they once did, the question then becomes: Can we construct new, more reliable measures of the kind of economy we now have?

We can with the power of modern computers. Like any change, a new way to measure our economy will be resisted. Charges will be leveled that the books are being cooked. When I entered the banking business, earnings were reported before allowance for loan losses. Citibank started to publish its reserve figure—an innovation at the time—and then instituted the concept of reporting earnings after allowing for loan losses. At the time, both initiatives were roundly condemned by our fellow bankers, although today both are standard. Just as each line in the federal budget has a political constituency, so also do various political and business groups have a stake in how our GNP is measured. The problem of changing yardsticks will always be more political than technical.

Some of our trading partners, however, are already moving in this direction. Japan proposed in January 1989 that the Office of Economic Cooperation and Development (OECD) change the way it measures economic performance.

Less reliance should be placed on the traditional measures, such as trade and budget figures, and more on spending on research and development, the extent of overseas investment, the ratio of high-tech industries to service companies, changes in industrial structure and labor mobility, the productivity of labor and capital, and the contribution of newly developed businesses.[6] Yet even a corrected set of traditional measuring sticks for the national economy might not be as relevant as they once were precisely because they are strictly national in scope. Once that was appropriate. Today, however, the global marketplace has moved from rhetoric to reality. National economies are no longer islands but, rather, an integral part of a larger global market.

In practice this fact of life is often overlooked. In 1972, for example, when U.S. imports as a percentage of the GNP were only about one-half as large as they are today, many forecasters underestimated the sharp increase in inflation that would follow the devaluation of the dollar that year. Other nations whose livelihood has depended on trade for years were not surprised.

The Netherlands, with a population about the size of New York State, although it maintains its own GNP accounts, knows full well that any sensible analysis of that nation's economy must proceed by looking at the rest of Europe as well. What is obvious about the Netherlands is true of the United States. It makes little sense today to use the GNP of the United States as presently computed.

For instance, for much of the 1980s economists predicted that the federal deficit would absorb so much of our domestic savings as to "crowd out" private investment. The crowding-out theory was never validated—the 1980s saw a powerful increase in U.S. business investment—because the theory ignored the reality of the global market. The proponents of the theory added up all the capital instruments sold on Wall Street in a year and then took the amount of federal debt sold and computed a ratio that purported to say that the federal government absorbed some significant percentage of all capital raised. That ratio may once have been useful, but today Wall Street, while still integral, is just one part of the global market. If foreigners choose to give up their currency to buy dollars to invest in America, it is not an act of charity but a hardheaded decision that they can do better here than at home. While still huge, American capital markets are only one international option for raising money. It is a matter of complete indifference to the chief financial officer of any major company whether one sells capital notes in New York, Hong Kong, or London. Decisions are made on the basis of rate and availability, not geography.

These tight linkages make an awareness of the growth rates of our major trading partners ever more essential to U.S. prosperity. Policies aimed at giving the GNP of the United States a short-term boost while ignoring possible global impacts are even less well advised today than they were sixty years ago, when a binge of protectionism helped bring on the Great Depression.

As the reality of the global market sinks in, policymakers from different nations will come to understand that even the strongest sovereign cannot entirely control its own destiny but will increasingly be forced to cooperate on economic issues it once regarded as almost exclusively national concerns. This in itself will force it to reexamine the ways it measures its national economies and may well spark a vigorous international effort to assemble more meaningful data on the world economy. The suggestions of MITI to the OECD, referred to earlier, is a first step in this direction.

The global economy may also prompt some increase in international economic regulation and even some more forceful attempts at international economic planning and manipulation. However, as we shall see in greater detail in later chapters, the barriers to procrustean government regulation in the information age are substantial. Moreover, however intensely nations cooperate in search of better data, they may never be able to measure certain economic phenomena with the apparent assurance with which we once measured the industrial economy.

In recent years we have witnessed furious, often partisan, debates about two leading factors in America's struggle to remain economically competitive: capital formation and productivity. Of both it has been said with great confidence that they were lagging and soaring, that they represented the light at the end of the tunnel, and that the light at the end of the tunnel was an oncoming train. The truth is that the information economy has made both far more difficult to measure. Assets recorded on today's balance sheets tend to be things we can feel and touch. On the accountants' ledgers the intellectual capital a company acquires tends to be treated as an expense, not as a real asset; it is not carried on the capital accounts along with the shiny new company car or the aging brick factory building, though neither contributes as much to the enterprise's productive capacity.

The magnitude of the resulting distortion is suggested by the fact that the world software market in 1989 was estimated to be between $50 and $60 billion and growing at about 15 percent a year.[7] As far as the accountants and economic statisticians are concerned, this $50 or $60 billion has almost disappeared into thin air. Companies expense most of the software when they buy it, and it appears in total on nobody's balance sheet as an asset that is in fact used on a daily basis.

If the software sold by IBM and thousands of other software producers suddenly disappeared, factories would stop running, accounting and payroll systems would cease to function, all the telephone switches would freeze, airlines would stop flying, and the economy would halt. It is hard to imagine such a vital business asset being virtually unrecorded anywhere, but that is the case.

If capital is what produces a stream of income—and that is a definition no one seems to quarrel with—then it follows that software is a form of capital. It has always been difficult to measure any form of knowledge capital, but in the past the problem was not as urgent, since the ratio of difficult-to-quantify knowledge capital to more tangible capital was not as high or growing as rapidly as it is today.

This development throws a different light on the problem of capital formation. To enter a business, the entrepreneur in the information age often needs access to knowledge more than he or she needs large sums of money. To write a software program that might make its author millions of dollars may require only a relatively trivial investment (enough to purchase a personal computer or at least rent time on a mainframe) compared to the investment needed to enter, say, a manufacturing business producing a comparable stream of income. It is the knowledge capital accumulated in the software writer's head or in the documentation or on disks that makes possible the new program. This capital is substantial and very real. And it does not show up with any clarity in the numbers economists customarily quote about capital formation.

The trends that are making intellectual capital an increasing proportion of national wealth are accelerating. At least 80 percent of all the scientists who ever lived are now alive. In our country at least half of all scientific research done since the United States was founded has been conducted in the last decade. With the total stock of our knowledge doubling about every ten or twelve years, it is clear that our intellectual capital is being formed far more rapidly than tangible capital.

Even the numbers we use to describe tangible capital investment are sometimes misleading. The figures may show that we are "disinvesting" when what we are really doing is paying less money for much more capacity. We see this in the ratio of price to capacity in the hand-held calculator or the watches on our wrists or the personal computers on our desks. They cost less than they did a few years ago. But they do more and by any reasonable standard represent an increase of capital. The intellectual value-added in a microchip far outweighs any cost of labor and materials. Experience shows us that the information economy drives down manufacturing costs (as compared to capacity, not units) at a pace that seems far faster than typical during the industrial era for the simple reason that as information products are refined, they rapidly gain capacity without increasing in size, cost of materials, or labor. The entire Industrial Revolution, says Dr. Carver Mead of the California Institute of Technology, "enhanced productivity by a factor of about a hundred." But "the microelectronic revolution has already enhanced productivity in the information-based technology by a factor of more than one million—and the end isn't in sight yet."

In doing their capital accounts, accountants have traditionally equated cost and value. This was a sensible procedure in the past, when the intellectual value-added in most products constituted a relatively modest proportion of the cost of labor, materials, and machinery, and the prices of products therefore fell at the relatively slow pace allowed by the industrial learning curve.

Imagine what this truth would mean for automobile manufacturers if, over the course of a few decades, without increasing the price or size of a six-passenger car, they could figure out how to make it hold 600 people, travel safely at 5,500 miles per hour, and get 2,600 miles to the gallon! That is roughly what has happened in the computer industry.

Nor are these considerations limited to stand-alone calculators and computers. As we saw in chapters 2 and 3, the microchip and other information technologies are everywhere. The usefulness of traditional capital accounting is being undermined by the spread of information into nearly all the "hard" products of our age.

At Citicorp, I encountered a perfect example of how the current vocabulary of economics and business describes a world that still exists in part but fails to capture the essential dynamics of this new world. My Citicorp colleague John Reed invented for us the term "investment spending," a concept it took us some time to understand because it seemed, at first glance, to be a contradiction in terms. But it was, and is, appropriate to our times. Simply put, in an information-based economy much of what we now consider expenditure—staff, software, or marketing programs, for example—is actually capital investment: It produces a high return and is self-financing.

Almost every day brilliant young scientists and engineers are hired by business enterprises for a fraction of what it cost American universities to produce them. Of course, even toting up the true dollar cost of their educations would fail to measure the contribution of the uncounted intellectual capital (retained intellectual earnings, as it were) accumulated by the universities over the years.

In early 1990, Intel Corp., one of the most important commercial enterprises of the information age, announced yet another of its stunning breakthroughs in information technology. Intel made fundamental advances in "data compression" technology that allows huge amounts of data—words, numbers, or pictures—to be transported from place to place in a fraction of the time currently required. Two-hour movies can be sent to your home in minutes; masses of data can be dispatched without tying up expensive circuits. The new technology will create enormous value for any enterprise, from the movies to modern medicine, that depends on real-time management of very large batches of complex data.

This new development will produce a stream of income, though river or tidal wave might be more accurate. Yet what economist would volunteer for the job of quantifying the intellectual investments responsible or figuring the return on investment? To be sure, Intel has been a research-based company since its inception and could show hefty expenditures in that regard. But the essential base of knowledge capital could not be contained or counted within the walls of Intel or even inside the borders of Silicon Valley. What is the knowledge capital base at Cal Tech or MIT or at the other universities that helped make Intel what it is today? How much capital did they form last year? What income will that capital produce? When will its effects be measured in the economy? Impossible-to-trace intellectual investments add more value to the economy almost overnight than years of carefully retained money earnings and cautious expansion in physical-plant improvements.

As the percentage of "knowledge workers" to manual workers increases, the difficulty of measuring productivity grows proportionately. The debate over the status of American productivity has been much in the news. How does America stack up in the global marketplace? Is the growth of American productivity greater or less than that of other nations? These are important questions, but once again, what do the words mean? Productivity, in the simplest terms, used to mean output per man-hour. While that was a useful concept in manufacturing, do we really have any meaningful measure of productivity for this information-intensive age when the vast majority of our workers are employed in the knowledge or service sectors? Current methodology, although quite sophisticated, fails to supply really meaningful numbers in many instances.

The huge and growing financial service industry is one example of the difficulty of measuring productivity. Once we get past counting the number of checks cleared per hour or the number of insurance claims paid—all of which display greatly improved productivity, thanks to the computer—we then move immediately into the realm of the subjective. Is a loan officer's productivity in a bank, an insurance company, or a credit company to be judged on the number of loans made per day? The size of the loans? The number of loans that are repaid on time? The quantity of bad debts created? How do you measure the productivity of workers who make such critical judgments? No one really knows, though many have tried.

The challenge of measuring productivity is spreading to

the industrial sector as information supplements, and in some cases replaces, physical capital. As Shoshana Zuboff and others have pointed out, management's usual first impulse has been to assess the productivity of factory automation almost exclusively by job reductions. But as her ambitious study *In the Age of the Smart Machine* demonstrated, even in enterprises in which automation was well handled, job reductions often fell short of expectations. The remaining workers, however, began to make new contributions to customer needs, including more reliable quality and faster and more conscientious service. Such improvements would not necessarily show on the books in a timely or easily quantifiable manner, though making great medium- and long-term contributions to the enterprise.

As Zuboff also points out, in a well-automated environment (and badly automated ones still seem to predominate in this new world) workers are enabled to more fully comprehend the productive process and take on more responsibility for it. That presents a challenge to middle managers, who rightly feel that their traditional roles are being taken over in part by automated scheduling and task-assignment systems and in part by self-policing workers themselves.

The best managers look for new ways to add value to the enterprise, and the others eventually follow along. Yet if these managers do begin to add value in thoroughly unexpected ways, how accurately will this phenomenon be represented by productivity statistics? Will the raw numbers reveal the history of productivity growth or obscure its true resources? And how many speeches will politicians have made in the meantime about declines in productivity because they were looking at old numbers, not new realities?

As information applied to work adds value to every aspect of economic activity, the problem of assessing productivity spreads throughout the economy. As long as we are unable reliably to quantify the productivity of knowledge workers or information technology, statistical alarms or number-crunching boasts about American productivity will have little credibility.

It will take a long time to construct a new measuring system for our global economy. When we achieve this goal, many will no doubt dismiss the results because they will be different from our current system in the great tradition of those who dismissed the accuracy of water clocks that did not agree with sundials. Nevertheless, until we do construct a new system, we may never again have such comfortably reliable statistical measures of the productivity of people or investment as we had in the past. The firm statistical measures of the industrial era may have been an artifact of their time. So how will we judge what course to take? Deprived of truly relevant numbers, we may have to substitute judgment plus a healthy dose of modesty, a combination sometimes called common sense.

For governments, the difficulty of quantifying intellectual capital or productivity will mean that they, too, will have to fall back on common sense, including an extra-large dose of modesty. Grand dreams of planned economies hail from an era in which government economists, like the accountant who opposed the Brooklyn Bridge because there was plenty of room on the ferry, used to be pretty sure what made economies work. They were usually wrong, but they were sure that their view of reality, derived largely from statistical pictures of the economy, was correct.

As we move into the information economy, that certainty will erode, at least for a time. Our statistical portraits may have to owe more to the impressionist school than to academic realism. Governments that value prosperity will have to give up their dreams of economic fine-tuning. You cannot fine-tune (if you ever could) what you cannot measure. Not all or even most political leaders will want to admit this. But these difficulties will be one more force arrayed against government manipulation of the economy, and it is only reasonable to expect them to have some effect. It will become essential for governments to recapture the wisdom of Socrates: to know that they do not know.

For governments, common sense in pursuit of prosperity may mean less fiddling with the details of economic output and more hard work on input, particularly of the human variety. The quality of education may be the most important way government can address productivity. Peter Drucker has called information the "primary material" of the new economy. If Marx were alive today, he might fairly call education the means of production.

If we are to compete in a global marketplace, we must constantly build and renew our intellectual capital. We have little or no control over the natural resources within our borders, but we do have control over our educational and cultural environment.

Our success in achieving outstanding agricultural productivity was not unrelated to our educational structure. When Abraham Lincoln signed the Morrill Act in 1862, the first land-grant colleges were formed offering courses in agriculture, engineering, and home economics. Some years later, in 1887, the Hatch Act expanded the program with federal funds for research. The county agent was the conduit of the new technology from campus to farm. And the United States, in large part as a result of such efforts, gave birth to the green revolution.

Soshana Zuboff observes that a key factor in determining whether workers succeed in realizing the full potential of information systems is their ability to master the technology and use it to create unexpected value rather than passively serving it. But this mastery requires workers to operate on levels of abstract and symbolic thought that may never before have been required in their jobs. It can be done, even by workers who never expected to evolve out of the blue-collar tradition. These new "intellective" skills, as Zuboff calls them, can be learned. But poorly educated workers, with minds untrained in and unchallenged by the abstract skills of math and science, who lack the confidence to learn the new system behind the new technology, are much less likely to meet the challenge.

Although much has been written about the decline of American competitiveness, in many ways this new global market plays to our strengths. The constant in the global marketplace is change, and change is what we Americans deal with best. We have always been innovators. Who else would choose as a national motto on our great seal *"novus ordo seclorum"*—the new order of the ages. This native adaptability is in itself a kind of "infrastructural" advantage, an infrastructure of culture that will serve us well as long as we refuse to panic in the face of statisticians and pundits wielding yesterday's numbers and telling us we're washed up if we remain ourselves.

In a time of often confusing transition, our goal must be to make common sense the order of the day. We must tell the politicians and pundits to stop flogging us with increasingly meaningless numbers. The governments of the world must drop the pretense of being able to outguess a world market that was always too complex to accommodate the pretenses of economic planners and which now less than ever can fit into any central plan or "industrial policy." But we can help our economic position by doing what we know is right: nourishing the growth of intellectual capital and shunning superstitious reverence for materialist totems of a bygone era.

CHAPTER SEVEN

SERENDIPITY, INC.

We are limited, not by our technology, but by the
way we think. We still think just the way we
thought two hundred years ago, as if nothing had
happened.

CARVER MEAD

POUL ANDERSON, ONE OF OUR MOST THOUGHTFUL WRITERS
of science fiction, imagines in one of his "future histories"
an interstellar consulting agency called Serendipity, Inc. With
the aid of the most capacious computer in the galaxy, Serendipity sells only one thing: information about potential
opportunities in distant solar systems. Serendipity does not
sell to the general public. Its only clients are an elite cadre
of space pioneers, traders, and adventurers who in the course
of their own travels pick up unique and timely bits of information about the remote reaches of the galaxy. Much of this
information, though not relevant to their own enterprises,
could be enormously profitable to others in a different line
of business.

In exchange for a deposit of such fresh information and an
enormous fee, the Serendipity computer will provide for a
client the exclusive information on some far-flung opportunity tailor-made for the client's own capabilities. But, and
here is the most intriguing part, the client does not ask the
computer any specific questions, for any subject about which

he knows enough to ask is probably too widely known to justify Serendipity's enormous fee. The whole point of the computer is that it has access to vast and obscure realms of knowledge of which the client knows nothing. The client simply tells the computer about his company's interests and resources. The computer then selects the single galactic opportunity for which the client is best suited and tells him what he needs to know to pursue it, without fear of competition, since no one else will be sold the same information.[1]

Anderson was imagining a future time in which information is the most valuable of all resources. That time is now, and Serendipity, Inc. and its clients, however fanciful, are in a very real way models for business corporations under the information standard. In their corporate strategies and structures, and even in their relationship to the state, Anderson's creations reflect the transforming power of the Information Standard.

When information technology made information the most important factor of production, it made the timely acquisition of the best information the number-one goal of business management, as it is for Serendipity and its clients. Information technology is simplifying corporate structure: The layered hordes of middle management whose primary function was once to move information up and down the corporate hierarchy are disappearing; at Serendipity the computer has replaced them entirely. Finally, no government bureaucrats regulate Serendipity or its clients. For one thing, the government neither knows nor understands what Serendipity is doing. Even in our own time, the paradigmatic information industries, such as microelectronics, remain largely unregulated because their technologies change too fast for any regulatory agency to keep up. Moreover, such industries are not only led but staffed at almost every level by knowledge workers who bridle at the idea of outsiders and amateurs from the government interfering in their work.

The supremacy of the sovereign state depends to some extent on the exercise of that power over lesser institutions. The most important of these institutions in a market economy is the business corporation. As the information standard changes the business corporation, it will change the sovereign state itself.

Information technology is changing the "government" of businesses, upsetting the "sovereign" privileges of top business executives and the traditional roles of middle managers and both traditional and professional workers, spreading corporate democracy, and making corporate subjects into corporate citizens.

This is a sea change from the time the large business corporation first appeared. Until recently, corporations have been organized along the same lines as the largest and most complex state organization: the military. The branching hierarchy of the military bureaucracy, which was essentially a communications system, and the tradition of following orders without question fulfilled the army's primary management goal: to make all the parts of a vast body respond as one to directions from above and to funnel intelligence smoothly in the opposite direction. One person can personally command or communicate with only so many others. As a result, the system developed into a hierarchy, replete with sergeants directing squads, lieutenants directing a platoon, captains directing a company, and so on up the line to the commander in chief.

By the end of the nineteenth century, the growing size and complexity of industrial organizations demanded similar coordination. The assembly line that vastly increased the flow of products per worker also greatly increased the need to manage and coordinate those workers: Middle management was born. Like sergeants, captains, and lieutenants, these men and women were skilled messengers bearing information up and down the line to keep the systems running smoothly. They had to make sure that the right part reached the right place at the right time, or else the process would break down.

The railroads provided an early example of modern business organization. Some attribute this to the fact that in the early days the railroads hired a great many men from the army corps of engineers to help them build their system and that they brought both their engineering knowledge and their organizing skills to the business. As trains began to move at speeds far beyond human experience, the roads were plagued by accidents. Railroad management responded by establishing chains of command at least as strict as those of a military unit. With the aid of an indispensable telegraph system, trains could be kept on schedule and out of danger.[2] The system did more than prevent accidents; it became a vast and systematic management tool. Managers throughout the railway system were required to file detailed and standardized daily, weekly, and monthly reports on traffic, maintenance, costs, etc., a real innovation at the time. The system certainly helped keep track of cars and freight and made it possible for the roads to use their resources sensibly. But it also shifted power up the hierarchy in the direction of those receiving the reports and reduced the autonomy of those below. As James R. Beniger writes:

> [The Western Railroad] programmed its operating workers with "careful and explicit rules." Enginemen, for example, became little more than programmable operators, dutifully following rules like "in descending grades higher than 60 feet per mile passenger trains are not to exceed 18 miles per hour and merchandise trains not over 10 miles per hour". . . [The] conductor . . . had standardized detailed programs for responding to delays, breakdowns and other contingencies . . . carried a watch synchronized with all others on the line, and . . . moved his train according to a precise timetable.[3]

These conductors, lower-echelon managers, were largely information carriers. So were the station and district managers. Indeed, not only in the railroads but throughout the industrial economy moving information was once the main task of most people dignified by the title of manager. Now we move most of it by machine. As Beniger points out, the conductor in many ways functioned as an on-board computer system. Today for many purposes he has been replaced by one.

Long before computers, the exquisitely organized management hierarchy of General Motors helped it dominate the automotive industry. A human information feedback system, starting at the dealer level, allowed the top management of the largest industrial corporation in the world to revise its production decisions every ten days. The industrial-era assembly line stayed in sync through the efforts of an army of clipboard bearers, grandly called managers, who constantly checked that the right parts and workers were in the right place at the right time doing the right things at acceptable levels of quality. Even mid-nineteenth century factories, few of which came close to fulfilling the assembly-line vision, required vast information systems consisting of whole corps of managerial workers that had never existed before.[4] Middle managers were unknown in the United States before the mid-nineteenth century, yet managers and clerks accounted for almost 17 percent of the U. S. work force by 1940. From 1900 to 1910 the number of managers in the U. S. work force grew by 45 percent, far outpacing the growth in the general work force. In the same decade, the number of stenographers, typists, and secretaries, the staff workers for middle management, increased 189 percent.[5] All these people shared essentially one function: to carry information up to decision makers and then carry the decisions back down.

Those at the top of such a classic industrial hierarchy might fancy themselves Napoleons of commerce, sole owners of the big picture, whose commands, conveyed eagerly by hundreds of white-collared subalterns, would turn squadrons of marketeers on a dime or unloose a devastating barrage of production. That world is vanishing.

Computers offer a hydraulic of the mind that frees us from

much of the drudgery of information processing in the same manner a bulldozer frees us from much of the drudgery of dirt processing. When the drudgery vanishes, however, so do many of the drudges. The man with the clipboard is gone from most shop floors; the computers keep track of parts and people. In sales, the managerial hierarchy is being flattened as men in the field file orders from their laptop computers directly to the company's mainframe. Staff and field managers whose job it was to present periodic pictures of the state of the business are disappearing because the state of the business is available to anyone with access to the computer.

Management layers that were set up to report rather than produce are beginning to disappear, changing the power structure of companies. The middle managers who used to convey information and the upper managers who "owned" it and held power thereby are losing that power and in some cases their jobs. The new information systems flatten the management hierarchy. They change the very meaning of management and the skills needed to do it well.

In the future, what will managers do? The answer is both simple and unsettling: They will run the business, which is what they should have been doing in the first place. Managers, no longer forced to devote most of their time to acquiring or moving information, will be able to use information to solve business problems.

What will this look like, practically speaking? Many managers will find it looks disturbingly like work. For instance, more and more managers are spending time outside the hierarchy, working in ad hoc groups formed to solve specific problems, rather than in routinized information management. Typically, these task forces are composed of specialists in various phases of the business: accounting, legal, marketing, manufacturing, and technical. Quite often they are formed to fix a problem and are dissolved when the solution is found. The members of the task force operate more like professional workers, who offer their own particular skills to

115

an operation, than like managers, who are defined by their place in the structure.

Years ago, when Castro seized the assets of American banks in Cuba, Citibank had a task force in place to do several things: to see that Americans got out of Cuba safely, that Cuban assets in the United States were identified and arrangements were made to seize them in satisfaction of debts due, to advise foreign correspondent banks of loss of control of the Cuban branches, to cancel test words and codes, to advise government agencies, to pass the proper accounting entries, and to take appropriate legal action. With all this done, the task force was disbanded, leaving behind a record of things learned for the next emergency. At the time, this was unusual enough to be noticed. Today it is becoming business as usual.

As the distinction between managers and professionals breaks down and managers do more professional work and spend less time facilitating the functioning of the corporate hierarchy, more and different types of people become eligible for leadership. It used to be all but axiomatic that the best loan officer in a bank would be groomed for the bank presidency. The credit function is still crucially important and must be always nurtured. But in a modern bank it may be more important to have as president the man with the best grasp of the information technology that allows banks to offer customers a range of services and options never previously imagined.

The new business organization will demand different leadership skills. Hierarchical organizations provide tight control of a large group of workers by placing relatively small groups of workers, or submanagers, under the direct supervision of a higher manager. Thus, the steepness of the management pyramid. Flatten that structure and the people within it get a lot less direct supervision. It becomes more important for organizations to have well-understood common goals by which workers can direct themselves. The job of instilling such goals has more to do with persuasion and teaching and leadership than with old-style management. Successful business leaders are finding that the skills of a good political leader are more relevant than those of the general.

Peter Drucker has compared tomorrow's business leader to a symphony conductor, and it is a good analogy:

> In some modern symphonies, hundreds of musicians are on stage together and play together. According to organization theory, there should be several "group vice president conductors" and perhaps half a dozen division VP conductors." But there is only one conductor—and every one of the musicians, each a high-grade specialist, plays directly to that person, without an intermediary.[6]

The erstwhile commanders, moreover, are finding yet another new challenge to their leadership: As information becomes the most important factor of production, good workers and managers must acquire more of it. Former subalterns become formidable experts with specialized skills that may outstrip those of the boss. These people reject autocracy because their talents cannot be efficiently used under the "command and control" model.

In her book *In the Age of the Smart Machine*, Zuboff dramatically illustrates the changing meanings of corporate power, management, and leadership by telling the story of how full computer automation came to two traditional paper mills and failed in one but succeeded in the other. Both mills had long been run by a corps of middle managers who supervised blue-collar worker-operators. The operators had spent most of their time moving about the plants checking on individual processors, vats of pulp, drying rooms, etc., developing a keen intuitive sense for how to keep them working at their best. Only the managers, however, knew what was going on in the plant as a whole: Given production and other goals by their bosses, the middle managers used the operators as tools to control the plant and meet the goals.

117

After automation, however, the operators spent most of their time in a central computer room from which they could operate most of the equipment. But that central computer room also gave the operators a chance to get a far better sense of overall plant operations, to learn for themselves what only the managers had known before. Soon the computer system was enhanced with a cost-control program that helped to do what managers had once done: adjust the manufacturing systems so as to meet cost and production goals.

The result, in both plants at first, was that many managers began to feel uneasy. They feared for their status and even their jobs, viewing the operators as competitors and even enemies. In the less successful plant these anxieties dominated: Managers chastised for laziness operators who made good use of the computer instead of sticking with "real work." Managers tried to keep information from operators, discouraged them from taking on new responsibilities, or refused to share their expertise. Morale suffered, workers began to shy away from learning the system, and automation fell far short of its goals. As one worker complained to Zuboff: "[The managers] don't want us to know very much, and the more they keep us in the dark, the more they can order us around."[7] An engineer from the same plant agreed: "They tend to try and keep the operators in the dark as a form of job security."[8] And upper management was indeed considering whether many of the middle managers might have become obsolete.

At the more successful plant, however, some middle managers did find a new and genuine role: that of teacher. The operators, after all, were blue-collar workers whose main tools had been experience and intuition, not the abstract skills demanded by the new system. They needed teachers.

The managers who understood this and worked to become teachers got the most out of the operators and were happiest with their jobs. As one particularly eloquent operator told Zuboff: "In a traditional system managers are drivers of people. You focus on driving people to work as hard as possible.

With our new technology environment, managers should be drivers of learning."[9]

We do not now generally recruit managers for their teaching ability. But as information becomes an ever more essential ingredient of production, teaching will become one of the most important management skills. To become more productive, companies must turn more laboring workers into knowledge workers. To do this we will have to tell managers "right out loud" that teaching is part of their job. They will have to adopt for themselves a teacher's ethic in which the greatest triumph is to be surpassed by one's student. Losing the old power of closely held knowledge, they must learn to cherish the new power of those who spread knowledge. One manager Zuboff interviewed learned this lesson particularly well:

> In this environment, the key to influence is not telling people what to do but in helping to shape the way they interpret the data. For example, in our unit, information is available to everyone, but I am the only one who can interpret it. I can either give them the result of my interpretations, or I can show them how to interpret it. If I choose the latter, I increase my influence. *Now there are fifteen people who think like I do.*[10]

The successful teacher-manager creates a new challenge for himself: leading men and women who have to a considerable extent become his peers. A company in which the vast majority of employees have become knowledge workers cannot be managed in the same way as a company of laborers. Organizing, even regimenting, the industrial work force was a great achievement in its day, making possible the assembly line, mass production and distribution, and fantastically productive economies of scale. But the work required of today's workers depends too much on creativity, autonomy, and personal judgment to be successfully regimented. Obedience to instructions was a great virtue in the industrial laborer, but

119

mere obedience, which is what the managers wanted in the unsuccessful mill, wastes and frustrates the potential of information technology. As Zuboff writes, in an information industry "internal commitment and motivation replace obedience. . . . As the work that people do becomes more abstract, the need for positive motivation and internal commitment becomes all the more crucial."[11] It is relatively easy to monitor whether a machine tender is working hard and well. Workers who work by thinking cannot be as easily monitored. They must be motivated, well taught, and engaged.

The fruits of this change will be tasted not only by the business organization but by the entire society and the sovereign state itself. A work force on the Information Standard will require more sophisticated corporate leadership; a nation composed largely of information workers will require the same. As more people become information users and fewer do jobs that can be comprehended by the military model of management, we must expect the rise of a work force that is better educated, more independent in judgment, more conscious of the value and bargaining power of its knowledge, and less willing to fit itself in to an aging power structure.

In the industrial age, work taught men to make themselves interchangeable parts in vast organizations not only in the factory but in the union, and even in the political organizations that claimed to represent the common interests of common men. Under the Information Standard men are likely to be less deferential to their former corporate sovereigns. But will a society of men and women who have learned that deference is due to knowledge rather than rank find it easy to defer to their *political* sovereigns, the regulators and would-be regulators of trade and technology, capital and labor?

It seems more likely that the regulators, usually a few steps behind in comprehending the onrush of new technologies and new opportunities, will find themselves gradually surrendering power, not perhaps over the essentials of public health and safety but over the details of enterprise. A nation of knowledge workers seems likely to regard the generalists who inhabit our legislatures and administrative agencies in the same light as they would managers who tried to substitute rank for knowledge in running their shops.

The information corporation makes colleagues and citizens, not subalterns and subjects. In societies already free and democratic the fathers and grandfathers of these men fought to strengthen the power of government in the hope of checking the abuse of workers who had little leverage beyond that provided by numbers, courage, and good organization. But they themselves will fight to reduce government power over the corporations for which they work, organizations far more democratic, collegial, and tolerant than distant state bureaucracies inhabited by men and women who never seem to have enough knowledge to temper or justify their power. In the burgeoning number of societies only now tasting or preparing to taste freedom and democracy, the change will be even greater. The bureaucrats in these lands are even less informed and far more powerful and destructive. Consequently, there is so much more to be gained by breaking their power, and much more exertion is necessary to achieve this goal.

This change in the internal power structure of the business corporation is not the only new challenge the corporation presents to the prerogatives of the sovereign state. The emerging business corporation not only transmits information more efficiently within the ranks but does a much better job capturing and capitalizing on information resources from all sources. Information technology makes the business environment far more competitive and unsettling, speeding up the "creative destruction" that Joseph Schumpeter identified as the essence of capitalism, doubling and redoubling the rewards of innovation or the prize for getting right information at the right time.

Sovereign governments, so often hostile to innovation, may try to frustrate such opportunistic organizations. But in the ruthless competition of an information economy, the successful corporation will become far more difficult for government to control.

The job that Poul Anderson's Serendipity computer performed for its clients—sorting out opportunities from an overwhelming flow of information—is now the prime mission of every good corporate management. True, under the Information Standard, information remains a management tool, but it is also a great deal more. Information is the raw material of wealth and opportunity. New scientific discoveries and technical capabilities provide a wish list of ways to add value to matter. Within new demographic, sociological, marketing, and economic data are hidden endless ideas for products, services, and marketing strategies. The knowledge explosion is an explosion of opportunities.

But how do we turn wish list into reality? Today more than ever, having a business strategy means having an information strategy, a strategy for recognizing opportunities in the onrush of change, a strategy for transforming data flows that now look like a necessary evil into new products, services, and sources of profit, a strategy for ensuring that a company derives full value from the knowledge accumulated by its workers rather than allowing that knowledge to languish or leak away.

Consider computerized airline reservation systems. American Airlines' Sabre system, by getting there first with the most enhancements, captured the lion's share of travel agents' computerized reservation business. But American went further. It built a data base of frequent flyers and used that information to develop not only marketing strategies but the American Airlines Advantage program as well. Today every major airline has a similar frequent-flyer program. They are so common we forget that they are the by-product of hundreds of millions of dollars and many years of effort spent to build huge data bases that in the first instance served another purpose entirely.

The essence of an information strategy is to turn the burden of burgeoning business data into a bounty of business opportunity. The business organization has to be rebuilt around the goal of managing information productively. The object of the game is to get information to the person or company that needs and can use it in a timely way.

Ian Sharp has built a data base in Toronto containing information about every commercial airplane that has flown in the United States during the past decade and a half. There are seventy pieces of data about each flight, ranging from time of takeoff and landing to number of passengers carried, yield per passenger, fuel consumed, and time and distance of flight. Sharp's data base can provide a crucial advantage for an airplane manufacturer contemplating a new design. With Sharp's data the manufacturer can now target specific routes, building planes of appropriate size, fuel economy, speed, maintenance requirements, etc. The estimations can make the difference between selling many planes or none. Knowing the market is what it is all about.

Over 90 percent of American goods now have a Universal Product Code, those familiar black stripes commonly known as a bar code. The checkout scanners that read those codes are creating a staggeringly informative, brand-new data base on what products are sold, in what volume, from what shelf, in what store, to what kinds of people. The long-term impact of this kind of data is still unclear, but we do know that as stores get a more detailed picture of their own customers, they are beginning to use more in-store advertising, "narrowcasting" their sales pitches to their prime audience rather than broadcasting to a less well understood audience through traditional media.

The banking business for generations depended on the loan officer's knowing more about his customer's needs and capabilities than other people did. This comparative advantage permitted the bank to lend money with a solid expectation that it would be paid back at maturity. But in the information economy, 10K reports have become available on tape from the SEC (Securities and Exchange Commission), and Dow Jones, Reuters, and the rest started keeping everyone up-to-date in real time. Software packages promising to make anyone into an expert financial analyst flooded the market.

In this environment an individual bank loses much of its comparative advantage. Soon the treasurer of General Electric knew as much about the credit of General Motors as did a bank lending officer. A new flow of information created a new market for commercial paper: corporations selling their unsecured notes directly to other corporations and bypassing the banks. Today the volume of commercial paper outstanding exceeds the total of commercial loans at all the New York banks put together.

As "copyrights" on business information break down, the manager will continue to shift away from procuring and carrying information to using it. New managers will be recruited for these new skills, but it is also important to reeducate older managers, who in a frantically innovative economy may "age" before their time. Today's businesses do devote an enormous amount of time and energy to executive reeducation, sponsoring hordes of conferences and executive retreats to consider new possibilities and chew over common problems. Many companies also hold such conferences for customers so that both sides can learn together how they can get the most from their relationships. Joint design efforts by customers and suppliers are in fact becoming more common, shortening delivery time, preventing costly first-time mistakes, and lowering costs. These conferences not only absorb considerable effort and expense; they are tantamount to admitting that thinking is work, always a hard point for management to concede but crucial in today's world.

We cannot, however, deal with the new opportunities of information simply by encouraging manager make-overs. The organizations people manage must be made over as well. Flattening organizations and squashing hierarchies simplify and shorten information pathways, making it easier for the right information to get to the right person at the right time.

As we have seen, information technology itself can flatten organizations and focus a company's intellectual resources. The former chief scientist of IBM, Dr. Ralph E. Gomory, told me that when a software writer gets stuck for a solution to a problem, he or she may "post" the problem on IBM's electronic bulletin board, which can be accessed by thousands of IBM employees all over the globe. The bulletin board often elicits an answer overnight from a fellow programmer thousands of miles away.

Many of our most innovative, fastest-growing companies tend to be "flat" by definition: they are small and often built around a few key pieces of information. Most of the growth, new jobs, and new ideas in the American economy come from small, innovative firms—that is to say, from companies that have created new information. In such firms employees tend to understand and share the company's goals, and information pathways are usually uncomplicated.

In the most advanced, high-tech sectors of the economy, this "entrepreneurial flattening" has been vindicated repeatedly. In the microelectronics industry, new and profitable information is created at a stunning rate. Yet older and larger firms (which in this sector may mean firms that have reached the ripe old age of fifteen or twenty years) have frequently been unable to capitalize on new technologies spawned in their own labs. The numerous Silicon Valley spin-off firms represent the sobering truth that the information pathway from the older company's lab to the venture capitalist's may be shorter and easier than the path to the company president's ear.

More than ever it has become important to recognize opportunities early. Yet as business and government bureaucracies expand and age, they tend to develop a kind of administrative arthritis: They move more slowly and are less agile in responding to market demands. Examples abound.

The commercial banks should have invented the credit card, but they did not. Kodak, which is almost always at the forefront of technology, was a natural to produce the first instant camera, but it was Dr. Land of Polaroid who brought the idea to market. General Electric should have been the world leader in electronic computers, but it was IBM, without a single electronic engineer in 1945, that saw the opportunity and seized the lead. The list of good companies that turned down the Xerox process reads like a who's who of American industry.

In each of these cases, companies with vast stores of expertise and information capital proved dull students of opportunity. The corporate graveyards of the world are littered with other companies with impressive, indeed intimidating, "technology assessment" programs loaded with experts but cut off from marketing people. Edison dismissed the phonograph he invented as an instrument of no commercial value.

Similarly, most of the management information systems (MIS) that exist today are too narrowly focused on the company itself. They are good for measuring a steady state of business but fail to tell us what we need to know to prosper in rapidly changing markets. Jack Kilby, who, along with Robert Noyce, has been credited with inventing the integrated circuit, is quoted by T. R. Reid as saying:

> At first, the problem solver has to look things over with a wide-angle lens, hunting down every fact that might conceivably be related to some kind of solution. This involves extensive reading, including all the obvious technical literature but also a broad range of other publications—books, broadsides, newspapers, magazines, speeches, catalogues, whatever happens in view.

In the same way, internal MIS systems must be integrated with external market data if they are to be really useful. One new tool that helps do this goes by the name of electronic data interchange (EDI). EDI ties business customers and supppliers electronically, automatically informing them about each other's current needs, inventories, prices, etc. Today about 70 percent of the Fortune 500 companies are using EDI both on the buy and sell side. It is estimated that in the wholesale drug industry customers transmit 95 percent of all their purchase orders to manufacturers via EDI. The major automobile manufacturers all use it, and IBM is seeking to connect two thousand of its largest suppliers. All of the information handled by EDI can be integrated with the manufacturing process to support highly efficient just-in-time inventory and production processes. Altogether such systems provide enormous data bases that must be integrated into our formal information systems (just as the value of such a valuable instrument of business must begin to be accounted for in our GNP).

The need for formal information systems, the need to flatten business organizations, the need to reeducate managers, all arise from the competitive imperatives of an information-rich, and therefore *innovation-rich*, economy. Nations that wish to flourish in such an economy will have to foster a climate of innovation. But allowing maximum freedom to innovate may upset traditional sovereign prerogatives. Many of the innovations of the information age, for instance, present significant challenges to seemingly long-settled law and custom. Is a computer terminal a branch of a bank? That is an important question for states in which sharp limitations on branch banking have been a cherished institution for generations. How do we protect intellectual property in the age of the Xerox machine, the VCR, and direct dialing to most places in the world? Who owns and assigns the radio frequencies of the world? How should the two hundred slots in the geosynchronous belt be allocated and by whom? International law and the laws of nations are being repeatedly challenged by onrushing technology. To the extent that U. S.

law fails to allow businesses to take full advantage of new information and new technologies, the United States will certainly lose some of its competitive edge.

Competition under the Information Standard will force companies to develop just those qualities that make them hard for governments to control. They will be international. They will be built to respond quickly to new opportunities. They will be well informed, more expert in their fields than their competitors or their regulators, and able to exploit new productive capabilities before regulatory bureaucracies can fully comprehend them. Because the bulk of their capital will be intellectual, they will be highly mobile, sensitive to their political and social environments, and always ready to shift operations to countries with more favorable climates. Indeed, as we shall see in the next chapter, the richest and most powerful nations of the world are already losing some of their traditional advantages in the global competition for infor-mation leadership.

CHAPTER EIGHT

BORDERS ARE NOT BOUNDARIES

> Radio waves have never respected frontiers, and
> from an altitude of 36,000 kilometers, national
> boundaries are singularly inconspicuous. The world
> of the future will be an open world.
>
> ARTHUR C. CLARKE

O N OCTOBER 4, 1957, I HAPPENED TO BE IN BAGHDAD, AN area in which an advanced civilization existed as early as 4000 B.C. But never in that long history had there been a day like this. On that date, the world was startled to learn that the Soviet Union had successfully launched Sputnik.

World reaction to the event was mixed. Dr. Edward Teller opined that the United States "had lost a battle more important and greater than Pearl Harbor." Dwight D. Eisenhower, the president of the United States, took a more sanguine view:

> So far as the satellite itself is concerned, that does not raise my apprehensions, not one iota. I see nothing at this moment . . . that is significant in that development as far as security is concerned, except . . . it does definitely prove the possession by the Russian scientists of a very powerful thrust in their rocketry. . . .

The military, represented by Rear Adm. Rawson Bennett, told an NBC television audience that Sputnik is "a hunk of iron almost anybody could launch." The chancellor of West Germany, Konrad Adenauer, related the event to European geography: "Five hundred and sixty miles is only the distance from Bonn to Vienna. It does not prove that they can fire anything parallel to the earth over a distance of many thousand miles."

The blinding clarity of hindsight shows us that Dr. Teller was in some ways closer to the mark than the military or our elected leaders. On the other hand, the fallout from the event did galvanize American politicians to mount a program that would put a man on the moon.

Satellite technology changed the world forever. Even today the full consequences have not yet been played out. These satellites now bind the world in an electronic infrastructure that carries news, money, and data anywhere on the planet with the speed of light. Satellites not only carry television, radio, and telephone transmissions around the world, but in so doing have for better or worse radically altered the "balance of information power," tipping it away from the state and toward the individual.

Of course, satellites are only part of the story. An onrush of technologies—the convergence of computers with telecommunications, VCRs, electronic data bases, ever cheaper and simpler techniques for collecting and broadcasting the news, and the fax machine—has created a global arena of shared popular information that takes no notice of the lines on the map. While some tens of thousands of financial specialists now have instant access to economic and financial news, hundreds of millions of people around the world are plugged into what has become essentially a single network— albeit with local interests and subdivisions—of popular communicaton. Today, for example, the 60 million personal computers in the United States can store, manipulate, and transmit information across myriad networks to other computers and to thousands of computer bulletin boards around the nation and the world. All kinds of special interest groups use these electronic boards to post their message. The *Los*

Angeles Times, for example, reported on April 24, 1988, that Amnesty International's action center, which alerts the world to gross violations of human rights anywhere in the world, is actually run from the home of a couple in a small town in Colorado. In addition to posting all kinds of information on bulletin boards, the personal computer (PC) puts huge mailing lists in the hands of political activists—and the mails are flooded with tens of millions of mailers promoting one cause or a candidate for office. No longer does it take a massive investment to produce a newsletter or a small newspaper. Desktop publishing technology gives small groups and even individuals that ability for around $20,000. In a kind of an electronic throwback to America's Committees of Correspondence during the Revolution that kept patriots advised of the latest developments in the war with England, private PC users have put in place thousands of electronic bulletin boards that carry news about everything from personal experience to political messages. The political power that can be mobilized against sovereign governments by the users of these electronic bulletin boards was demonstrated, ironically, when in 1987 the Federal Communications Commission (FCC) suggested that telephone rates be raised for computer network users. According to the *Wall Street Journal*, Congress and the FCC were inundated with mail protesting the proposed rate hikes. Although the journalist Bob Davis headlined the article "Hobbyists as Lobbyists," these networks are now used by professional pressure groups of all kinds and are capable of burying congressional mail rooms on any given issue.

The radio talk show host is another wild card in the efforts of sovereigns to put their spin on government news. An issue like a tax increase, for example, which in former days might have snuck through the local council, can become a hot issue when the citizens call in to express their views, egged on by the master of ceremonies. This is a new phenomenon in America that appears further to weaken any chance a sovereign has to contain news of an unfavorable event.

Indeed, Orwell's vision has been reversed: Instead of the sovereign hearing each word said by a citizen in the privacy of his or her home, it is the citizen who hears what the sovereign is doing and has myriad electronic pathways to register approval or dissent. All of a sudden, everyone has access to everything, except in the most primitive regions or in those countries whose leaders are so dedicated to repression that they are willing to cut their nations out of modernity to maintain their rule. But as we saw in Romania, particularly, such rulers are fast disappearing.

All of this has profound effects on the ancient concept of sovereignty. The sanctity of national borders is an artifact of another age. Today data of all kinds move across, over, and through those borders as if they did not exist. Over the horizon radar reaches deep into "national" airspace of the largest countries, and satellites look down with high-resolution cameras at installations hidden deep within national borders.

Borders are no longer boundaries; technology has made them porous. More than that, since satellite communications are now non-Euclidean in the sense that the communication distance between all points covered by a satellite's footprint are basically equal, borders are no long partitions between one area and another.

A historian of the Left, E. J. Hobsbawm, describes the current scene this way:

> At present we are living through a curious combination of the technology of the late twentieth century, the free trade of the nineteenth, and the rebirth of the sort of interstitial centres characteristic of world trade in the Middle Ages. City states like Hong Kong and Singapore revive, extraterritorial "industrial zones" multiply inside technically sovereign nation-states like Hanseatic Steelyards, and so do offshore tax havens in otherwise valueless islands whose only function is, precisely, to remove economic transactions from the control of

nation-states. The ideology of nations and nationalism is irrelevant to any of these developments.[1]

History is replete with efforts by governments to control, channel, or obliterate information. In most countries in the West, the postal and telecommunication businesses are owned and operated by the state. It is said that the English kings wanted the Crown to control the postal services so that they could steam open envelopes to search for treasonous material. The advent of the telegraph and its use by the press presented new and novel problems. Ithiel de Sola Pool tells us, "In many countries what developed . . . were concessionary telegraph rates. Where telegraph services were state-owned, the reductions were often massive and politically based. Governments were willing to suffer a loss to keep the political good will of the press and to gain some leverage over it."[2] This practice became obsolete when the news organizations built their own communication networks, and today very little news moves by commercial telegraph. But however transmitted, the printed press had a profound influence on the way society in general and nation-states in particular operated. Richard Brown has written:

> When the diffusion of public information moved from face-to-face networks to the newspaper page, public life and the society in which politics operated shifted from a communal discipline to a market-oriented, competitive regimen in which the foundations of influence changed. This did not happen everywhere all at once, or for every type of public information, but by the middle decades of the nineteenth century so much of public affairs was being conducted through the press that where extra-local public information was concerned, word-of-mouth networks had been largely relegated to a subordinate role.[3]

As each new medium came along, governments invented new mechanisms of control. In America there are three rather distinct standards that have been applied to three sectors of the communications industry. Broadly speaking, there is one standard for the printed press, one for broadcasting of all types, and one for common carriers, such as the telephone. The First Amendment has protected the print media in the United States not only to say what it wished but also from special taxes, any attempt at control through licensing, or even requiring the right to reply as now obtains in broadcasting.[4] The Constitution says that "Congress shall make no law . . . abridging the freedom of speech, or of the press." The court has taken the position that "no law" means just that.

Radio, on the other hand, is replete with rigid rules that are anathema to print journalism. These restrictions rest on the theory that the airwaves are public property and the broadcaster a trustee who is thus subject to regulations ranging from the prohibition of broadcasting pornography to the guarantee of the public's right to reply. Broadcasting, both over the air and via cable, is also often subject to special taxes or fees, the imposition of which have been ruled unconstitutional with respect to the print media.

Telephones, as common carriers, have still a different set of regulations regarding everything from access to their lines to the confidentiality of the data that travel over its wires or microwaves and even to what other businesses a common carrier company might enter.

The increasing convergence of the technologies currently powering broadcasting, publishing, telephones, and cable will pose problems for the sovereign undreamed of when the technologies first appeared. The three regulatory models are basically incompatible, and as the technology merges, it is probable that the First Amendment model will prevail as the operative policy, and so the power to regulate the other models must decline.

The United States, despite its commitment to the expansion of freedom, has never put much money behind its efforts to tell the story of freedom around the world. Since national budgets often reveal national priorities, the U.S. budget is instructive in this regard. As late as 1987 the line item in the federal budget for military bands was $154,200,000, while the budget for salaries and expenses of the Voice of America was $169 million. Some nations put a much higher value on the war of words crossing borders and resort to jamming broadcasts in order to block out even the modest effort the United States has made to tell the story of freedom. Such censorship is prohibited by international law. Article 19 of the Universal Declaration of Human Rights provides: "Everyone has the right of freedom of opinion and expression: this right includes freedom to . . . receive and impart information and ideas through any media and regardless of frontiers." This principle is also articulated in the Helsinki Agreement of 1975. Despite these agreements, many nations do not want their citizens to hear other views, and they jam outside radio broadcasts.

The Soviets, for example, explained their jamming by saying they were mindful of a 1936 treaty—the International Convention Governing the Use of Broadcasting in the Cause of Peace. This old League of Nations product was designed to stop Nazi propaganda aimed at Germany's neighbors by Hitler. It is a prime example of hard cases making bad law.

As information moves financial markets, so also is it altering the political structure of the world by invading local political contests without the consent of the government involved. Some years ago, Ferdinand Marcos was elected president of the Philippines and took office without incident. In the 1986 Philippine election the television cameras went into the barrios, and the whole world knew the election was fraudulent. Despite Marcos's assertion that he won the election, world opinion, enforced by the instant flow of information, forced him into exile.

In another part of the world, a different technology was

used to unseat a shah. In a sense, it is ironic that a would-be leader of one of the lesser developed countries first grasped the potential political power of the audiocassette. Close observers assign some measurable part of the success of the revolution perpetrated by the Ayatollah Khomeini to his skillful use of such cassettes, recorded at his base in France, smuggled into Iran, and broadcast to the people.

All new technology tends to erode the influence of existing power structures. The current attack on the power of sovereigns is the proliferation of knowledge that used to be confined to small groups of leaders but is now popping up on screens all over the world. When a monopoly of information is broken, the power structure is in danger. This is true across the human spectrum, from societies dominated by witch doctors to the most sophisticated governments. A rudimentary knowledge of medicine broke the power of witch doctors, and the growing knowledge that freedom exists in other areas is toppling some repressive governments. The geosynchronous satellite that broadcasts news to people with hand-held transistor radios gives citizens of closed societies a basis for comparing their lot to others. This is a clear and present danger to dictators of all kinds.

The first reaction of those in power is usually to ignore a new technology, but then, if it persists, to denigrate its usefulness and, finally, to embrace it in an attempt to maintain power. And yet even as they attempt to maintain their power by embracing the new technology, the elites can find themselves altered by it. Some may survive the change, but their position and function in society even within the ruling class will be changed. Modern information technology is so powerful politically that elites who embrace it will be altered beyond recognition. And yet those who utterly reject it will condemn their countries to second-class status or worse.

The Communist grip on Eastern Europe was broken not by violent revolution (except in Romania) but by what can only

be called a political surrender of the ruling elites, a surrender
that in several cases involved a public confession of failure
by party hierarchs. In Communist show trials of the past,
fallen apparatchiks also made confessions, pleading guilty to
utterly fantastic accounts of their supposed crimes as if to
honor the power of the state to control history itself. Yet
this time around the failed leadership confessed not to a
state-conjured tale of horrors but to the simple reality of
communism's failure. Political leaders confessed to what
everyone knew, in large part to demonstrate to their former
subjects that they were sufficiently in touch with reality to
merit some future role in the governance of the nation. They
joined in the national conversation and were changed by it.

Jeane Kirkpatrick has written:

> The speed with which the Soviet Union and Eastern
> Europe were transformed was itself a great shock. A
> chief characteristic of Marxist-Leninist states had al-
> ways been the skill of their elites not only in seizing
> and consolidating power but also in preserving power.
> None had ever been overthrown by its own military,
> although several existed in countries with a tradition
> of military coups and intrigue. None had ever fallen
> because of dissension in its ranks, although several were
> found in countries with a tradition of factionalism.
> None had been overthrown from within nor evolved
> into any other kind of government, although several
> existed in countries where there was a long tradition of
> regime instability. These regimes were called totalitar-
> ian because they claimed total jurisdiction over all as-
> pects of the society.[5]

In lands where the big lie was at once both creed and litmus
test, a display of power and a demonstration of the political
effectiveness of terror, it is now simply ridiculous. The first
requirement of any aspiring leader in the new Eastern bloc is
that he or she publicly reject the lies of the past. Even politics
in the former Soviet Union has already become democratic

in this one sense: It is performed in an arena of shared information acknowledged by all rather than in a political theater of the absurd in which frantic denial of reality was the essential motif of the drama. That arena of shared information is a creation of information technology. As the Iron Curtain has become porous to ideas, information, and even entertainment, the Communist elites have been unable to convince even party members to stick to the party line.

In short, politics, even in the East, is subject to the information revolution. Information has always been a key to political power. But when information abounds and overflows in public, when an entire society is privy to what once may have been closely guarded "secrets," political strategies based on a close holding of information no longer work. When everyone in the nation, at least potentially, can join in a single national "conversation," there are only two ways, as we have seen, in which a government can keep its power: It can allow its policies to be guided by that national conversation or it can revert to a level of repression that even totalitarian regimes find inconvenient in the best of times and which in an age of instant information brings world opprobrium.

There was more behind the liberation of Eastern Europe than a revolution in technology. Sheer brutal terror, such as we saw in Tiananmen Square, might have stopped it and was nearly tried in the Soviet Union in August 1991. Nevertheless, information technology and the emergence of an international Information Standard in politics played a powerful role. And as events progressed, the revolution was spread largely by the power of television and radio as the citizens in each of the bloc states were given hope by the pictures of progress next door.

The latest example of the power of the information revolution is the world reaction to the plight of the Kurds after the Gulf War. Although the Kurds have been subjected to subjugation or attempted subjugation for centuries—at least since the seventh century, when Kurdistan was conquered by the Arabs—their plight never attracted the attention of the world until vivid images of starving children appeared on television screens around the world. While the principle of noninterference in the internal affairs of a sovereign power has long been a tenet of international law, the television images of these pathetic children swept it aside, and allied forces eventually were forced by public pressure to go into Iraq to protect the Kurds and feed the hungry. Indeed, serious students of international affairs have begun to question the concept of what constitutes "internal affairs" and to suggest that the international community had an "obligation" to intervene in defense of human rights anywhere in the world, national borders notwithstanding. This new dialogue is driven by the information revolution, which brings human suffering thousands of miles away into our living rooms, but is a long way from the traditional concept of sovereignty.

Because the power of the First Amendment here in the United States is so great and our tradition of free speech so powerful, Americans rarely contemplate the political power of information. Yet even in the home of democratic rights, the United Kingdom, information has not been as free as one would think. "For 50 years," writes Rupert Murdoch, "British television has operated on the assumption that the people could not be trusted to watch what they wanted to watch, so it had to be controlled by like-minded people who knew what was good for them."[6] By way of contrast, in America the choice is huge; nearly 60 percent of American homes have cable television, carrying about two dozen channels at a cost of approximately fifteen dollars a month. Mr. Murdoch went on to say: "This compares to a compulsory £66 license fee in Britain, which brings you two channels, whether you want them or not."[7] But the lack of choice is only one problem. There are political consequences as well.

British broadcasters are now constantly subject to inhibiting criticism and reporting restrictions. BBC staff have even been vetted by government security forces. . . . Enormous pressure succeeded in stopping a programme on Count Tolstoy's book about British involvement in the forced repatriation of anti-Communist Russians and Yugoslavs after the war. In another era, Churchill's warnings on the dangers of Hitler were kept off the BBC to please the Chamberlain Government.[8]

As more and more competitors to BBC come in—and with satellite technology they cannot practically be stopped—this kind of thing will become increasingly impossible. Tyrants and their subjects know most about this power. The control of information was the bedrock of both Communist and Nazi regimes. The Soviets for decades devoted enormous resources to controlling not only radio and television, printing presses, or photostat machines, but even mimeograph machines.

Though we in the United States have relatively little experience with systematic repression by the state of information, we certainly have seen power structures upset as the flow of information became more bountiful. Perhaps the most dramatic example was the civil rights movement: The plight of black people in parts of our nation went almost unnoticed by many Americans for almost a hundred years. Suddenly the TV cameras brought into our living rooms the image of Bull Connor with his dogs and whips. Americans decided together in very short order that this was wrong, and the civil rights movement made a quantum leap forward and dramatically changed the political landscape in our country. Politicians were quick to understand what was happening, and some tried to hold back the tide of images cascading on the American public. A well-known Mississippi state senator by the name of Wilburn Hooker succeeded in getting a law passed in that state setting up an "electronic curtain" to shield the citizens of his state from outside radio and TV reports on the civil rights movement. The attempted information blockade was, of course, totally ineffective. For one thing, Mississippi lacked the technical ability to jam broadcasts. Despite these efforts, television made the conditions of blacks under Jim Crow part of the common national conversation. Once that happened, the civil rights revolution was almost inevitable.

"Information blockades" are becoming impractical everywhere, not just in open societies such as ours. Borders are no longer barriers to information. And where there are no effective borders, the concept of what constitutes sovereignty begins, by necessity, to alter.

The breakdown of borders to information is not simply a matter of raw technology. There is already a world market in information, including powerful and increasingly international enterprises that effectively subvert government power even when they intend to do nothing more than entertain or inform a worldwide audience. U.S.-made television programming, for instance, has become steadily more available around the world and seems to be in ever greater demand. Even in China after the repression signaled by Tiananmen Square, millions of people are still watching *The Sound of Music* and *Patton* for entertainment. Coincidentally, they are learning about other ways of life in other parts of the world. Just as the escalating costs of high-tech product development drive companies to exploit global markets more aggressively than ever, the escalating costs of television production have driven U.S. producers to market their products aggressively outside the United States. Revenues from first-season U.S. broadcasts are no longer sufficient to pay for any prime-time show, and producers now depend for their profits on domestic and foreign syndication revenues.

Because of this and because Hollywood still leads the rest of the world in the production of quality popular entertainment, all of Western Europe and much of the rest of the world avidly follow American prime-time dramas and situation comedies. The world buys eagerly in part because their consumers like American programming and in part because their own domestic markets are even less able than the U.S. market to provide sole support for local productions.

Currently, across Europe more than 70 percent of nondocumentary TV programming is imported, and more than 50 percent comes from the United States. European governments do not like this. France and Italy have been particularly vocal about a cultural invasion, and the European Community (EC) has approved a directive stating that European TV stations should devote a majority of their airtime to European-made programming.[9]

Yet any effort truly to control what the citizens of free European nations watch on television seems very likely to fail. SKY Channel alone, a satellite-based system, has more than 17 million viewers in Europe. If Communist governments cannot stop the flow of information at the border, it seems quite unlikely that the governments of free nations could take the measures necessary to keep "L.A. Law" off European TV screens. Indeed, some years ago the Danish government decreed that "Dallas" be removed from Danish TV as inappropriate entertainment for its citizens. This action created such a political firestorm from enraged citizens that the government had to bring back J. R. Ewing and his family to national TV.

Moreover, the issue is likely to become moot. Just as multinational corporations and transnational business alliances, once overwhelmingly an American phenomenon, have become the world's way of knitting together a global market, television, film, and other media production seems likely to go transnational as well. In fact, organizations such as the Associated Press and Reuters are among the oldest examples of major businesses pursuing a strategy of transnational business alliance. The Japanese have recently invested heavily in American entertainment companies. British and American coproduction and distribution deals are becoming much more common. Organizations such as News Corporation Limited, the company controlled by Rupert Murdoch, operate major print, broadcast, and film production companies on three continents and defy national classification. All of this private bypassing of borders is now supported by more than twenty-six thousand nongovernmental international business and labor organizations.[10]

If information organizations are going global, so is the information they offer. The "Americanization" of popular productions is already under way in Europe, particularly in England. If affairs follow their normal course, we in America will soon be learning from the Europeans and the Japanese as well as teaching them. This has already happened in other media. As Oswald Ganley has pointed out, it is not only *Time* and *Newsweek* that are read by decision makers all over the world but the *Economist* and *Paris Match* as well.[11] Elites in Japan, Europe, and North America are so thoroughly immersed in the same pool of information, entertainment, and even gossip that they have, according to Kenichi Ohmae, created a worldwide market in fashion-based consumer goods. These people really do live in a "global village."

The nations that are the mainstay of this global media village are also world leaders in personal freedom, particularly freedom of speech and the press. Although much is made currently of the dominance of Japan in many areas, some of the foundations of this power rests on the government's lingering ability to control the lives and life-styles of its citizens. This control is being eroded by the flow of information. Ohmae says:

> In Japan . . . our leaders can no longer keep the people in substandard housing because we know—directly—how people elsewhere live. We now travel abroad. In fact, ten million Japanese travel abroad annually these days. Or we can sit in our living rooms at home, watch CNN, and know instantaneously what is happening in the United States. During 1988, nearly 90 percent of all Japanese honeymooners went abroad. This kind of fact is hard to ignore. The government now seriously recognizes that it has built plants and offices but has failed to meet the needs of its young people for relaxation and

recreation. So, for the first time in 2,000 years, our people are revolting against their government and telling it what it must do for them. This would have been unthinkable when only a small official elite controlled access to all information.[12]

This flow of information will not only not disappear; it will increase. A new series of innovations in television broadcasting equipment is turning the entire world into a local news beat. So efficient an information pathway has television news become that TV has developed into a force in world affairs and a weapon of diplomacy. The national and international agendas of nations are increasingly being set not by some grand government plan but by the media: Policymakers have to spend a good share of their time and energy dealing with whatever crisis or pseudocrisis has been identified by the media that particular day. Real issues, deliberative thought, and long-range strategic plans are often casualties of whatever damage-control actions are required at the moment. In these circumstances, the old bipartisanship, at least in American foreign affairs, has fallen prey to a new divisiveness. The so-called TV docudramas, part fact, part fiction, have even attempted to change the record of past events. The merging of media and message has created a situation wherein, according to Daniel Boorstin, a "larger and larger proportion of our experience, of what we read and see and hear, has come to consist of pseudo-events."[13]

This kind of information is rarely a solid foundation for good policy judgments. However, it characterizes the age in which we live. We live in a world where Yasir Arafat works with a media consultant; where Mohammed Abbas, who hijacked the *Achille Lauro* and murdered an old man in cold blood, appears on American network television even though he was a fugitive from justice at the time; where the Iranians stage marches for the cameras; and where Soviet spokesmen appear regularly on American TV. The communications revolution has made today's world very different from that of Citizen Edmond Genet—now, instead of being asked to leave the country, he would be on Ted Koppel's "Nightline" to protest President George Washington's outrageous policies.

Without passing a value judgment on whether this is good or bad, the fact is that representative government, as envisaged by the Founding Fathers, is no longer operating in the manner originally intended. Every government in the world has had to change and adapt its way of governing because the use of information technology has far outstripped the political process.

Fernand Braudel has written that the sovereign's first task has always been "to secure obedience, to gain for itself the monopoly of the use of force in a given society, neutralizing all the possible challenges inside it and replacing them with what Max Weber called 'legitimate violence' "[14] The central government took over the private armies of feudal lords and city-states to create a monopoly of power. Today that monopoly is being challenged by new private armies called terrorists. And once again technology plays a role.

No one understands the use of information technology better than modern terrorists. The terrorists who stormed the American embassy in Tehran and held fifty-two hostages from November 4, 1979, to January 18, 1981, were equipped with their own television cameras and their own microwave linkups to Iranian TV. The world's media organizations were only too eager to give events in Iran saturation coverage. In fact, ABC's "Nightline," now a fixture of late-night news coverage, was created in order to cover the hostage crisis.

In June 1985 the world saw on their TV screens a TWA Boeing 727 on the tarmac at Beirut Airport with the pilot John Testrake, a gun to his head, being interviewed by a reporter as if the reporter were covering the events at a political convention. The fate of the passengers on this TWA plane absorbed more than half of the network news programs. In fact, William C. Adams, who made a study of the TWA coverage, says that the percentage of the evening broadcasts devoted to the story was between 62 and 68 percent. In a brilliant study called *Terrorist Spectaculars*, the journalist Michael O'Neill observes that

> ... the networks will be listed in the final ledger of consequences because they must share responsibility for what occurred. They were not just watchers, standing and observing, but card-carrying participants who helped shape and direct the unfolding drama. They merged with the crisis, became part of it, and action and coverage became so intertwined it was hard to tell one from the other. . . .[15]

There is no easy answer for this phenomenon, but there is little question that no matter what its propriety, it is here to stay. Former Secretary of State George Shultz has called terrorism "low-intensity warfare," but whatever it is called, it is a form of war against the citizens of some country that further impinges on what used to be sovereignty. And few would argue that, in Mrs. Thatcher's words, the media give the terrorists "the oxygen of publicity," presenting even more difficult dilemmas for sovereign governments in the future.

Recently, Gladys and Oswald Ganley published a study on the political implications of the spread of videocassettes. They concluded, among other things, that "despite widespread bans on both VCRs and videocassette programming, people globally are at present viewing almost whatever they choose to." They point out that cassette

> distribution has been greatly aided by widespread black markets, ample smuggling routes, organized crime groups, cassette pirates, large numbers of migrant workers, and a variety of (often hidden) discretionary income in theoretically poor countries. This is occurring despite hundreds of years of government censorship of other media in most nations.

The Ganleys expected to find sharp distinctions in how and to what extent VCRs and videocassette tapes had penetrated the free, Communist, and developing worlds. Instead, they found that videocassette piracy was "global," the smuggling of VCRs "omnipresent."

> Migrant couriers of VCRs and cassettes cross all sorts of world borders . . . illegal machines and tapes are bought worldwide, despite an apparent lack of income; and specific political acts using VCRs and cassettes have been discovered to have occurred in a wide variety of settings. Although VCRs and cassettes are often unwanted by governments, no government, including that of the Soviet Union, has been able to put a stop to them.[16]

The Ganleys, writing in the mid-1980s, before the apparent dissolution of Communist control in Eastern Europe, document a number of cases in which VCRs were used for explicitly political purposes in the Eastern bloc and show also that both machines and tapes were commonly available in most of the bloc countries by that time.

It is too early to assess whether or how much the VCR contributed to the upheaval in Europe, but we do know that dissidents used videotapes extensively and that the Communist government tried very hard to stop them. The KGB was concerned that videotapes would be used for *Magnitizdat*—a word coined for "tape publishing"—by political opposition groups. Their concerns were well founded. When Poland was under martial law during the early 1980s, Solidarity smuggled to the Western media videotaped interviews with outlawed Solidarity leaders. And because video is such a simple and inexpensive technology compared to film, the emergence of the VCR gave a great boost to underground moviemaking, both dramas and documentaries, many with political messages.

These technological developments profoundly affect the

political structure of the world and over time will help to expand human freedom. History teaches that revolutions occur when people become aware of alternatives to their lot. This is happening all over the world, and it appears to be beyond the power of any sovereign government to stop it. That is good news for those who believe in freedom.

All modern societies require access to huge amounts of information and must have the computer power to solve immensely complex problems. An open society like ours fosters the exchange of information. In the United States it is possible for a private citizen to access well over three thousand data bases, many from their personal computers at home. A closed society like the former Soviet Union, in which information was the monopoly of the state and where even the GNP (gross national product) until recently was a classified number, handcuffed itself out of existence. The Kremlin wanted to have the Soviet Union keep up with the West, yet it would not allow its people fully to participate in the information revolution. For if it had allowed that, it would have risked losing control of its information monopoly—which is in fact what happened. Modern scientific research increasingly requires the ability to have access to huge data bases at remote locations. If access is limited to a small number of scientists, progress will be slowed. Opening up data bases to large numbers of men and women loosens the state's control. It is a very real Hobson's choice, and the dilemma will only get worse over time.

Thus, as in the case of business regulation, government power over information is being mitigated in part by the need to compete with more free, less regulated nations and economies. In this regard, the contrast between the West and the East of course is quite stark. But even among the democratic capitalist nations a competition for freedom is emerging. One of the most striking examples of free governments asserting their control over mostly private communications has been state-licensed or state-owned telephone monopolies. The public ownership of the post office tended to carry over to the telephones as they came along; indeed, in most European countries the PTTs (postal telegraph and telephone administrations) are government monopolies. One might think that as long as governments did not engage in censorship, this was nothing more than a benign government utility. Such is not the case. The public ownership of the PTTs gave the government enormous power to frustrate powerful new telecommunications technologies, which has huge implications for the free flow of information, money, and electronic services. In addition ". . . PTTs insist on charging exorbitant rates for incoming and outgoing broadcasts."[17] In Germany, for example, in the mid-1980s, the Bundespost told the international news service Reuters that satellite technology would not work. After much negotiation, it was agreed that if Bundespost people installed the satellite dish on the roof of the Reuters building and connected it to their lines, they would give it a try. To no one's surprise, the satellite functioned perfectly. But much valuable time was lost. In a similar manner PTTs resisted intelligent terminals in the offices of their customers, preferring to keep the intelligence within their own system.

Control over the channeling of information—who learns about what and when—has always conferred power on both the controller of the switch and on the recipient. One of the early examples of this phenomenon occurred in a small town in the Midwest. Some readers probably remember the days when you picked up the telephone and it was answered by a human being who asked for the number, then plugged the cord from your phone into a hole on the switchboard connecting it to another phone. It was not entirely unknown for an operator to overhear some of the conversation. In the particular town I am thinking of, there was a man named Strowger who ran an undertaking business. He had only one competitor, but that competitor always seemed to get most of the business. It didn't take much detective work for

Strowger to discover the reason. His competitor's sister was the telephone operator. Whenever she heard of a death in the village, she switched the call to her brother, effectively cutting off most of Strowger's business.

In self-defense, Strowger invented a device to eliminate the human telephone operator. It was a ratchet-based electro-mechanical switch. When a spring was added to this device by a watchmaker, the invention formed the basis of the familiar dial on latter-day telephones. The switch and its successors fundamentally changed the telephone business and the way it was configured and managed.

Strowger's successors are thousands of technologists in hundreds of companies devoted to designing "value-added" telecommunications services, to strengthening and refining the vast telecommunications network that, as we have seen, is remaking finance, industry, and trade around the world. Yet state-licensed and state-run monopoly phone companies have always been a potential threat to these new technologies. In fact, the decade-long series of court cases that ended in the breakup of the Bell system and allowed for competition in many aspects of American telecommunications started with a fight over whether AT&T could prohibit devices not of its devising from being attached to the system.

Today Japan and much of Europe have started down the same road to privatizing and deregulating national phone systems. Progress is slow in some countries. But Japan and almost all the EC nations have recognized to some degree that too much government control over the phone system will hinder innovations and impose significant competitive disadvantages on their citizens. The old PTTs are gradually being exposed to competition and forced to pare back regulations controlling what their lines can be used for or what equipment can be attached to them.

Another facet of the reluctance of the sovereign to loosen controls covers national and international regulation of transborder data flow (TBDF), as the diplomats have learned to call it. TBDF has been defined simply as "the flow across borders of any kind of material that is computer readable." TBDF raises various concerns. Many governments have passed privacy laws regulating what sort of information about citizens may be kept in government or private data banks and under what conditions sensitive information can be sold or given to others. They wish to be able to extend these protections to data concerning their citizens but stored or transferred beyond their borders. Less noble motives also come into play, including protectionism.

Despite these powerful motives, not much has been done to effectively restrict TBDF. In part, this is because domestic businesses see such restrictions as a competitive burden. These companies oppose their own governments' regulatory ambitions. Moreover, regulating the flow of bits and bytes over a telecom network is pretty difficult without a massive system for decoding and reading the data, in effect the equivalent of steaming open electronic mail. In countries with a long tradition of privacy, such actions do not sit well with the populace. And finally, in nearly all these countries the tradition of free speech is strong enough to raise alarms at the idea of governments setting up "tollbooths" to collect a tax on the flow of ideas.

The media, which have no particular love for Wall Street and the financial service business, finally came to understand that the flow of electrons that carried their news stories was indistinguishable from the electrons that carried the general ledger of Citibank or Coca-Cola; thus, their interests in the unrestricted flow of data was one with those of business institutions. Once the issue of media "free speech" was joined, the momentum went out of the movement to find ways to block TBDF.

From TBDF between the developed market economies to illegal videotapes behind the Iron Curtain to openly received or secretly snared satellite TV transmissions around the globe, the moral is the same: Borders are becoming irrelevant to information, and yet borders as boundaries have been one of the pillars of the ancient concept of sovereignty. Borders have in fact defined sovereignty—until today. The information age is forcing a reexamination of what constitutes sovereignty. More and more we are learning that problems ranging from the world's ecology to the assignment of radio frequencies will be solved only with the sufferance or the cooperation of others, including other sovereigns.

In the world we are building today it is impossible to assert sovereignty over information because information and the pathways over which it travels, including the heavens themselves, are shared in common. It is increasingly difficult to keep one's citizens out of the global conversation. As Tolkien would say, "The road goes ever on and on." But on this road one travels at the speed of light down a million pulsing pathways, and the trolls are just not clever or quick enough to catch you.

THE GREAT EQUALIZER

Gentlemen do not read each other's mail.

HENRY L. STIMSON, secretary of state

INFORMATION HAS ALWAYS BEEN SOCIETY'S GREAT EQUALIZER. But the control of information is most important to the sovereign in the conduct of war. Advance knowledge of where the enemy is, in what strength, and with what intent has often changed the long odds of battle. The drive to obtain this information and the desire to keep it hidden form the history of cryptography.

Not surprisingly, it was the militant Spartans who established the first known system of military cryptography. David Kahn tells us:

> As early as the fifth century B.C., they employed a device called the 'skytale,' the earliest apparatus used in cryptography and one of the few ever devised in the whole history of the science for transposition ciphers. The skytale consists of a staff of wood around which a strip of papyrus or leather or parchment is wrapped close-packed. The secret message is written on the parchment down the length of the staff; the parchment is then unwound and sent on its way. The disconnected

letters make no sense unless the parchment is re-wrapped around a baton of the same thickness as the first: then words leap from loop to loop, forming the message.

This enciphering device is mentioned by Thucydides in describing how the rulers of Sparta ordered a too ambitious Spartan prince and general home in about 475 B.C. About a century later, according to Plutarch, another skytale message recalled the Spartan general "Lysander to face charges of insubordination. Xenophon also records the skytale's use in enciphering a list of names in an order sent to another Spartan commander."[1]

It is a long way from these primitive efforts to conceal information from the enemy to modern codes and ciphers. Though the technology has changed dramatically, the intent has remained the same: to read the enemy's messages and to keep one's own secret. In addition to the effectiveness of the code, the way in which messages are carried or transmitted from one place to another is an important element in the security of the system.

So long as military dispatches were hand carried, the enemy had to capture the messenger to obtain the message. This presented problems not only for the enemy in obtaining intelligence but also the home commanders as well: Events often moved faster than the messengers. Martin van Creveld wrote about the Battle of Coronea, which took place in 394 B.C. and "where news of a defeat came right in the middle of a ceremony in which the Spartan King Agesilaus was being crowned victor by his men." The speed and safety of communication were not the only difficult problems faced by the sovereign. Sometimes the messenger got through safely but unknowingly delivered his message to the enemy. This fact was well understood by commanders and played a role in the American Revolution. Barbara Tuchman tells us:

On July 28, de Grasse wrote the conclusive letter that was to reach Rochambeau and Washington on August 14 informing them that he was coming with 25 or 26 ships, bringing three regiments, and would leave on August 3 for Chesapeake Bay. Speeding directly by the *Concorde*, the letter did not pass through diplomatic channels to be read and copied by agents in English pay. . . . In the 18th century, the practice was customary. Foreign ministries maintained regular clerks, who, through long familiarity, learned the codes, and read and copied the correspondence of officials of foreign countries.[2]

While de Grasse and Washington managed to keep secret the news of the movement of the French naval and military forces and thus contribute significantly to the success of the American Revolution, some years later it was not secrecy but simply the slowness of a sailing ship bringing a clear text message that caused many men to die. On January 8, 1815, Andrew Jackson's army defeated the British at the Battle of New Orleans, an engagement that was fought more than two weeks after the Treaty of Ghent ending the war was signed. It is difficult in this information age to understand a time when it took up to six weeks for news to cross the Atlantic, depending on the wind. In more recent times, I happened to be at a White House dinner in May 1975 when the Cambodian government seized the crew of the American cargo ship *Mayaguez*. The crew was rescued by the U.S. Navy and Marines, and I inquired of an admiral seated next to me after dinner how long priority messages took to travel from Thailand to the Pentagon and was told that really urgent ones came through in six hours. Despite the message delays through military channels, it was possible for President Carter to have talked by telephone to the pilots of the helicopters in the aborted rescue attempt of American hostages in Iran.

Military commanders have from the beginning searched for faster and more secure ways to communicate with their troops. The first breakthrough came with the invention of the optical telegraph in 1794, which consisted of a series of towers, the signal flags or lights from one being visible to the next. This device greatly expanded a military commander's control over larger areas and speeded up the transmission of messages without greatly damaging security. It was this system of moving information that enabled Napoleon to maintain control over large areas of conquered territory. Today we have only the legacy of "telegraph hills" to remind us of what was once state-of-the-art information technology.

The invention and then the widespread use of the telegraph made military communications much faster and easier but also less secure than hand-carried messages. While wiretaps could produce some intelligence, they required agents behind enemy lines to attach the wires and then get the intercepted messages back to their own commanders. Radio finally gave military commanders what they had always sought—continuous and fast communications to control an entire army. It also provided the first sure and rapid way to communicate with air and naval forces. Like most technology, however, radio was a two-edged sword. Anyone, friend or foe, can tune in if he or she knows the correct frequency and has the proper equipment. Radio communication came into common use by the military during World War I and spawned the invention of radio-direction finders to locate enemy stations. Intercepting enemy messages became relatively easy. Thousands of intercepts piled up, but since most of the messages were in code, they were of little use unless their secrets could be unlocked. Only the French, with a tradition in cryptanalysis stretching back to the great Rossignol in the seventeenth century, were well prepared for this task. "One of the most important contributions of the Rossignols," writes David Kahn, "was to make crystal clear to the rulers of France the importance of cryptanalyzed dispatches in framing their policy."[3] Perhaps the most famous use of a deciphered message to affect global events was an encrypted message sent on January 16, 1917, by the German foreign secretary Arthur Zimmermann to the German ambassador to the United States. In it, Zimmermann said that in the event of war with the United States, Mexico would be promised the return of Texas, New Mexico, and Arizona for entering the war as Germany's ally. The code was broken by the British and the message forwarded to President Woodrow Wilson, who released it to the press on March 1, 1917. There is little doubt that this information helped bring the United States into the war.

Secretary of State Henry L. Stimson's dictum was discarded when war broke out, and black chambers were established on both sides of the battle lines in an effort to break the enemy codes and supply information to the military commanders. Indeed, this battle of the black chambers continues to this day. In World War II, the ability of American cryptologists to crack the Japanese code and thus supply vital intelligence to our naval commanders in the battles of the Coral Sea and Midway is generally regarded as one of the most significant factors in turning the tide of battle.

The breaking of the Japanese diplomatic and naval codes was all the more remarkable when one considers that the United States entered World War II with very little in the way of truly sophisticated ciphers. The mainstay for army divisional traffic was a Swedish machine invented by Boris Caesar Wilhelm Hagelin and given the army designation of Converter M-209. It was a polyalphabetic system that produced a printed tape, and because of inner workings, more than a hundred million letters could be enciphered before the mechanical sequence in the machine would repeat itself. Since the cipher's secret could be broken down given time, efforts were expanded to design a more secure system.

By the end of the war we were using an electromechanical device known as m-134-c, or SIGABA. This was a highly effective cipher machine. David Kahn writes:

> The branch of the Army's Signal Security Agency charged with testing American cryptosystems had failed in all its efforts to break down messages enciphered in m-134-c. And, though the United States did not know it at the time, German cryptanalysts had, despite prolonged efforts, likewise found it impossible to read these cryptograms.[4]

Because much of the traffic from Eisenhower's headquarters was on SIGABA ciphers, extraordinary security measures were taken to protect both the machine itself and the rotors that made it work. The machine was stored in one safe and the rotors in another. Just after war's end, I was the officer responsible for two SIGABA machines, sets of rotors, and accompanying manuals in a signal center in Cebu. It was a great feeling of relief when a newly minted second lieutenant showed up to sign for all this top-secret equipment and allowed me to go home unencumbered by the weight of that responsibility. And yet by today's standards, even this system was primitive.

As codes and code breaking have become more sophisticated, so also have the means of transmitting messages in wartime. These communication lines now stretch over huge distances. One recent example was the war over the Falkland Islands. The distance from Great Britain to the Falklands was almost eight thousand miles, and yet the British forces operating under strict rules of engagement were all directed from Northwood, England, the home of fleet headquarters. Contrast this with the fact that it took fifteen and a half hours from the time the United States intercepted and decoded the message to the Japanese ambassador to break off negotiations with the United States at 1:00 P.M. on December 7, 1941, until that warning was delivered to General Short in

Hawaii—about two hours after the Japanese attack on Pearl Harbor. Even perfect intelligence delivered too late is useless.

Today modern information technology has the capacity to furnish some battle information in real time. Knowing precisely where one is on a battlefield or in the air over enemy territory gives ground commanders and pilots a competitive edge in battle. This information was especially important in the Gulf War, which was fought in a trackless desert devoid of the usual landmarks. Allied military commanders and pilots were able to pinpoint their position by use of hand-held radio receivers picking up signals from our Global Positioning Satellite System. Using this information, pilots could approach at high altitude beyond the range of antiaircraft fire, and only when the system indicated that they were directly over the assigned target did they dive down to drop their bombs. In addition to knowing precisely where you are, knowing when and where the enemy is launching missiles can turn the tide of battle. In Desert Storm, a twenty-year-old Defense Support Program (DSP) satellite using infrared detectors that sense the heat from missile plums reported ballistic missile launches in real time. These same satellites can also "see" nuclear explosions anywhere on the surface of the planet.

In addition to precise information about their exact location, commanders have always wanted a panoramic view of the battlefield but have not always welcomed the technology that might supply it. The first attempts to obtain a "view" of an entire battlefield were made by hot-air balloon enthusiasts in the late eighteenth century. These early pioneers of flight attempted to sell the military on the usefulness of aerial observation of enemy action, but even so great a general as Napoleon failed to appreciate its usefulness. Military men have often failed to embrace new military hardware ranging from the battle tank to the submarine, and aerial observation was no exception. Alan Palmer writes that despite official discouragement, "Carnot encouraged the use of captive balloons for military reconnaissance as early as 1794 . . . and he subsequently attached an experimental balloon corps to the army in the field; but Bonaparte ordered the corps to be disbanded in 1800."[5]

Modern commanders take a different view and now rely on many kinds of airborne reconnaissance. The American Armed Forces use the Airborne Warning and Control System (AWACS), which provides extended radar coverage beyond the line-of-sight, horizon-limited surface radar. Indeed, the AWACS (E3-C Sentry), which is based on the Boeing 707-320B Airframe and is powered by 4 Pratt and Whitney TF 33 engines, when flying over France, gives the commander a view of almost the entire NATO (North Atlantic Treaty Organization) command area. The radar, which is built by Westinghouse, provides long-range surveillance by means of a large rotating radome attached to the top of the fuselage. This special radar, developed for the AWACS, has a "look down" capability that can "see" small, low-altitude targets in land and sea clutter.

Long-range surveillance is but one of the pieces of information that can be supplied by AWACS. The twenty-three-member crew, which includes thirteen tactical controllers as well as communication and countermeasure operators, has access to fourteen situation display consoles for airborne command and control.

Today the "look down" radar is being further enhanced by a major systems improvement program that is said to permit identification of cruise missiles and Stealth-type aircraft and even further ranges, approximately 290 nautical miles at 29,000 feet.[6]

The navy has a similar need for information that is supplied by the carrier-based E-2 Hawkeye developed by Grumman Aircraft. The surveillance radar, built by GE, is capable of detecting airborne targets anywhere in a 3-million-cubic-mile surveillance volume while at the same time monitoring maritime traffic on the sea. High-speed signal processing enables the E-2 Hawkeye to track more than two thousand targets simultaneously and to control more than forty airborne intercepts. A new version, the APS-145, will perform to even higher standards.

While these, and other aircraft with advanced pulse Doppler radar, track enemy targets with previously unheard of accuracy, the weapons are information systems in and of themselves. In at least one instance, it can be argued that a "smart" weapon was an equalizer between an illiterate Afghan tribesman and the might of the invading Soviet army. The weapon is called the Stinger; its basic ground-to-air version uses an IR (infrared) homing sensor, can be carried by one man, and is fired from the shoulder. The Stinger is effective against low-flying helicopter gunships as well as fixed-wing aircraft. It is a so-called fire-and-forget missile and carries on board a sophisticated information system to identify friend from foe. The IFF (Identification, Friend or Foe) system interrogates coded transponders on friendly aircraft. Recently there have been several upgrades of the basic Stinger, including POST (Passive Optical Seeker Technology) and reprogrammable microprocessor. The basic Stinger had a profound effect on the war in Afghanistan and also in Angola. Weighing 34.5 pounds, including the launcher, the missile uses a solid-fuel rocket motor. With an estimated effective range of two to three kilometers and a very high target interception rate, it was the nemesis of the Soviet attack helicopter in Afghanistan. For some time it was estimated that a Russian jet or helicopter was shot down each day with a Stinger. This devastating defense by the Mujahedin forced Russian aircraft to fly at higher altitudes, which hindered their effectiveness in ground support roles. It is probably not an exaggeration to say that not since the musket destroyed the once-overpowering firepower of massed bowmen has new technology performed such an equalizing role.

In the air, the first-known use of "smart" air-to-air missiles in combat occurred, Michael Fitzpatrick writes, in October 1958.

> U.S. supplied Nationalist Chinese F-86's downed fourteen Chinese MIG-17's . . . in a single day. A quarter of a century later, during the 1982 Falkland War, British Harriers routed Argentina's faster, French-built Mirage fighters, with nineteen "kills" in twenty-three engagements. . . . Also in 1982, during intense Israeli-Syrian fighting . . . Syria lost over fifty-five Soviet-built MIGs. . . . The missile that performed so well in each of these instances was the AIM-9 Sidewinder.[7]

Like its cousin, the Stinger, it relies on information technology for its effectiveness.

The equalizing effect of information technology was clearly evident in the seventy-four-day war between the world's third largest naval power, Great Britain, and a developing country, Argentina. The Ganleys summed up the situation this way:

> Argentina, with no weapons industry of its own to speak of, could challenge the quite powerful Great Britain because it had stockpiled large quantities of modern weapons from various Western countries. It had a small navy of old, but updated American-, British-, and West German-built ships and submarines fitted with modern missiles and torpedoes. Because of British nuclear submarine power, Argentina's navy was neutralized in this conflict. But at least six of its ships had French Exocet surface-to-surface offensive missiles and British Sea Cat missiles for surface-to-air defenses which would have been usable if circumstances had been only a little different. Argentina's land-based Roland missiles, which protected the Stanley Airport runways, came from France, and its tanks and tank guns had been designed in West Germany.[8]

With all the power of Great Britain, it still lost six ships during the war; it failed to find the larger Argentine submarines and was unable to put the Stanley runway out of commission.[9]

In October 1988, a paper was presented to the U.S. government by the Commission on Integrated Long-Term Strategy, which was chaired by Dr. Fred Iklé and Prof. Albert J. Wohistetter, that stated that "smart conventional weapon systems are one of several classes of military technologies with the potential to profoundly influence future warfare."[10] The report also stressed that "Nonmaterial factors—tactics, training, leadership, morale—are critically important."[11]

With these caveats, smart weapons are then defined: "The term 'smart' applies to weapons that receive information during flight—from on-board systems and/or external sources—to help acquire and select targets."[12] Any way that "smart" is defined, what it means in practice is some kind of an on-board information system. As in all things, what man invents man can counteract. If the "brains" of smart weapons are software, we are vulnerable to relatively cheap attacks on some of our most costly and complex weapon systems in our arsenal.

Work done by Scott A. Boorman, a Yale University sociology professor, and Paul R. Levitt, a mathematician, suggests:

> At a time when computer software is part of 80 percent of U.S. weapon systems now in development, software warfare—attacking the software that controls or operates these weapons—may be the most effective, cheapest and simplest way to cripple vital U.S. defenses. Software warfare in fact is coming of age as a new type of systematic offensive warfare, one that can be waged far removed in space and time from any battlefield to influence not only combat outcomes but also peacetime balances of power.[13]

Recently, computer "viruses" have been in the news. These "viruses" are actually a string or strings of computer codes that may lie dormant for weeks or even years until called to life and can then disrupt a computer system.

"Software attack, often best carried out with the aid of well-placed insiders, is emerging as a coherent new type of systematic offensive warfare," according to Boorman and Levitt, writing recently in the military electronics journal *Signal*. It can

> strike key civilian targets, such as electronic funds transfer, other financial and data communications, air traffic control systems and even the vote-tallying machinery at the heart of the democratic process.
>
> Tactics that can be used to disrupt computer operations include viruses, which clone themselves to spread to other computers; "Trojan horses," which look and act like normal programs but contain hidden commands; "logic bombs," which remain inactive until a certain result in computation; and "time bombs."
>
> The so-called "logic bomb," which was planted in the computer software of the Los Angeles Department of Water and Power in the spring of 1985, made it impossible for that utility to access its own files for a week.[14]

In today's world, wars can be won or lost in a week. If nothing happened when the president pressed the button, if all our communications froze and our radar failed to function, our defensive posture would change dramatically. It does not take much imagination—while the story of the John Walker family is fresh in our minds—to imagine that some software programmer might sell out to our adversaries and plant a few "logic bombs" to bring down our communications or disrupt our military guidance systems. When you compare the cost of software warfare with a new weapons system, it can only be described as incredibly cheap by any standard.

Unlike complex weapons systems, planting software time bombs or "viruses" is within the financial reach of the smallest countries and, if successful, is capable of altering military balance in a manner similar to the way the invention of new weapons has done in the past. The sabotage of algorithms, which discriminate enemy missiles from decoys, might well be the critical factor in a battle.

The British found out in the Falklands war that their software controlling the Sea Wolf missile system on British warships could not cope with two aircraft attacking along parallel flight paths. Since the system could not decide which plane to shoot first, it simply shut down. This was not sabotage, but an oversight in the software design, and is illustrative of the huge military cost involved if the system does not function in combat.

There have been cases of intentional software warfare. Scott Boorman has written about a serious case of software sabotage uncovered in the 1970s at a U.S. Army supply base in Taegu, Korea. A group of South Koreans and U.S. personnel manipulated the inventory program "to siphon off many million dollars a year—$18 million is one figure that has been indicated—worth of military supplies," according to Mr. Boorman.[15]

Another area of vulnerability can be in the computer chips themselves. Chips may be made that include listening devices. Often called Trojan horses, they can collect and manipulate data. Americans found this out the hard way in the construction of the American embassy in Moscow. Indeed, the *New York Times* reported in June 1987 that James Schlesinger, a member of the team that was sent over by the secretary of state to inspect the embassy, stated that "some of the bugs found in concrete parts of the building . . . were so advanced that American experts remain baffled as to how they are supposed to work."

It is not necessary to plant bugs in the walls to access the information stored in thousands of military data bases. While student "hackers" delight in accessing electronic bulletin boards and attempting to break into various data bases as a kind of intellectual challenge, sometimes these efforts take on a more serious coloration. In 1985 a hacker—who it turned out was in Germany—broke into the computer files at Lawrence Berkeley Lab and into dozens of military bases in the United States. Clifford Stoll, an astronomer who was assigned to a computer center at Lawrence Berkeley Lab, first uncovered the computer break-in through a seventy-five-cent accounting error that showed an unauthorized use of the computer. As the plot unraveled it led through computer networks around the world, and Clifford Stoll wound up telling his story to the NSA (National Security Agency), the FBI, and the CIA. Stoll traced the hacker to Hannover, West Germany, where it was subsequently discovered that he was selling information to KGB agents in East Germany. The hacker was actually several persons; all five were charged with espionage on March 2, 1989, by the German authorities.[16]

After tracking the hacker through thirty or forty computers, Stoll summed up his thoughts:

> . . . our networks seem to have become the targets of (and channels for) international espionage. Come to think of it, what would I do if I were an intelligence agent? To collect secret information, I might train an agent to speak a foreign language, fly her to a distant country, supply her with bribe money, and worry that she might be caught up or fed duplicitous information.
>
> Or I could hire a dishonest computer programmer. Such a spy need never leave his home country. Not much risk of an internationally embarrassing incident. It's cheap, too—a few small computers and some network connections. And the information returned is fresh—straight from the target's word processing system.
>
> Today there's only one country that's not reachable from your telephone: Albania. What does this mean for the future of espionage?[17]

While agents in place are still seen as an indispensable element in obtaining good intelligence, that agent might well be a computer programmer rather than someone from Smiley's world.

With so many ways for information to be obtained, efforts have been made over the years to find a way to send a message, the very existence of which is concealed. This science has been given the name steganography and includes everything from invisible ink to advanced electronic deception. One of the most effective ways to pass information is the microdot. This photographic process reduces the picture of a document to the size of a period on this page. The picture can then be placed unnoticed on innocent documents carried across borders and enlarged and read by the recipient. The same principle can be used electronically; messages are compressed and transmitted in a "burst" lasting a few seconds—too short a time, it is hoped, for the sender to be located by a radio direction finder. A similar technique is used to dilute the strength of a radio signal so that it blends with and gets lost in background noise. There is an almost endless list of electronic methods of steganography. One way among many was a system of rapidly changing frequencies, or as it was called, frequency hopping. This system appeared in the early 1970s when "TRW began designing a satellite system for use by the CIA in communicating with agents in 'denied areas.' "[18] Private designers of somewhat similar systems found that instead of the patent they had applied for, they received a secrecy order.

One day, Jack Scantlin, who designed the Citicard and the cash machines they operated, came into my office and asked what I was worried about that day. I told him that so much money was moving over the wire from London to New York, I was concerned that the circuit would be intercepted and the money diverted. The answer was obviously encryption, but most commercial devices were slow and not very secure. A few months later, my phone rang and a senior officer in the Department of Defense inquired whether I knew a Jack Scantlin. I told him I did, and he then said that Scantlin had

167

applied for a patent on a new cipher that the government did not want to see leave the country, so we never got to use the invention. While the secret war goes on between sovereigns, many have speculated that this government power will be turned against the citizen. Is there a kind of Orwellian plot by government to turn citizens into his character Winston, who lived "in the assumption that every sound you made was overheard"? The existence of that power has fostered a host of laws to protect the citizen against the state. Nevertheless, the NSA's desire to control the design of commercial codes raises doubts. Indeed, the debate between the NSA and commercial firms on types of ciphers that they can use still goes on. Part of that dialogue revolves around what kind of a "key" may be used, since one of the important factors in code breaking is the length of the key. The official government civilian cipher designed by IBM and in broad commercial use through the 1980s has a 56-bit key, although their original suggestion was for a 128-bit key. Obviously, a shorter key makes the cryptanalysis job easier. If it is too short, many believe that the NSA can easily read all messages originated by U.S. commercial firms, but if it is much longer and therefore more secure, officials worry about sending the technology overseas, where it might fall into the wrong hands. Once more the power of sovereign control is being attenuated by rapidly moving technology. While the debate goes on in the United States, Europeans are already using and selling far more sophisticated ciphers to anyone who will buy them.

All of these efforts and many, many more are designed by the sovereign to protect the secrecy of information and move it from here to there safely and in a time frame when it is still useful. Equally huge efforts are made to break the ciphers and code, intercept the messages, and get the information so revealed to policymakers or fighter pilots in time to be useful. This battle of technology was christened the "Wizard War" by Winston Churchill and assigned a crucial role in the Battle of Britain. The secrets of science ranged from Britain's successful black chamber to the development of radar and the jamming of German aircraft's nagivational devices. Missing from this chapter by Churchill is any mention of one of the great victories in the Wizard War: Ultra, the code name for the machine the British had constructed to read the German code, even though this was as important in winning the war as the American triumph in reading the Japanese code. Indeed, Ultra remained secret until 1974, and many intercepts have even now not been published. The crucial role of science was described by Churchill this way:

> Yet if we had not mastered its profound meaning and used its mysteries even while we saw them only in a glimpse, all the efforts, all the prowess of the fighting airmen, all the bravery and sacrifices of the people, would have been in vain. Unless British science had proved superior to German and unless its strange sinister resources had been effectively brought to bear on the struggle for survival, we might well have been defeated, and, being defeated, destroyed.[19]

In that great war, once again information was the great equalizer.

CHAPTER TEN

POWER TO THE PEOPLE

> A system of genuine people power is being created
> and the groundwork laid for building a rule-of-law
> country.
>
> MIKHAIL GORBACHEV

THE OLD REVOLUTIONARY CHANT "POWER TO THE PEOPLE," usually accompanied by a raised clenched fist, has gone out of fashion. The failure of the socialist model has become too evident. The phrase probably came from the battle cry of the Bolsheviks during the Russian Revolution when the slogan was "Power to the Soviets." In America in the 1960s the Soviet slogan was corrupted into what some called "participatory democracy," and people like "Tom Hayden of Students for a Democratic Society were calling for a transfer of power to the 'people,' whom they were able to identify as themselves."[1] Later on, the "Power to the People" slogan was adopted by Bobby Seale as the chant of the Black Panthers. Needless to say, the last thing many of these people had in mind was actually giving all of the people a real voice in their government. But that is what is happening now.

While this radical political movement has lost its momentum, the information age is rapidly giving the power to the people in parts of the world and in a way that only a few years ago seemed impossible. What has made the impossible almost inevitable is the technology of modern communications.

The degree to which people were isolated, one from the other, before the days of modern communication technology is hard even to imagine now. People still alive today in America remember well the advent of radio, which brought into the isolated farmhouse voices from far away, music to listen to, and plays and musicals to fill the home with a richness of information undreamed of by even the wealthiest potentate of former days.

Few people foresaw the impact of radio, and the concept that it would ever be used for entertainment developed slowly. Even so great a futurist as H. G. Wells believed it was a gimmick, a transient phenomenon at best. "I am reported to be pessimistic about broadcasting," Wells wrote, but ". . . the truth is that I have anticipated its complete disappearance—confident that the unfortunate people, who must now subdue themselves 'listening in,' will soon find a better pastime for their leisure."[2] In 1916, David Sarnoff sent a memo to his boss at Marconi Wireless Telegraph Company that read as follows: "I have in mind a plan of development which would make radio a household utility in the same sense as a piano or phonograph. The idea is to bring music into the house by wireless."[3] No action was taken on Sarnoff's memo, and it was left to Dr. Frank Conrad to launch radio entertainment more or less as a by-product of his experiments with wireless. He found there were a lot of people who "enjoyed listening to the phonograph records which he put on the air; and the Westinghouse people set up a station to provide such entertainment and thus stimulate the sale of sets."[4] Despite the complaints of wireless operators, radio caught on. The Democratic convention in June 1924 was carried live, and then two years later the first broadcast of a World Series game took place, an event heard by 15 million people. The world has never been the same.

Today radio is omnipresent, in many of its different forms, not only for news and entertainment; it has many other uses. There presently exists, as we have seen, a hand-held radio device that locks onto the transmission from satellites and identifies one's exact location on the planet within a few meters. This is a far cry from the year 1931, when one of the world's most exciting events occurred. A young aviator from Texas named Wiley Post and his copilot, Harold Gatty, flew around the northern part of the world in the amazing time of eight days, fifteen hours, and fifty-one minutes. In anticipation of the event, I had wound a coil on an old Morton Salt carton, obtained a cat's whisker and a crystal from a mail-order catalog, and borrowed a pair of earphones. With this crude homemade radio I sat in rapt attention as an unseen announcer described how Wiley Post brought his plane in for a landing at the end of his record flight. While the flight made history, it was the radio that brought the event to the attention of the world.

As men and women communicate with each other, either face-to-face or via satellite, all of the important relationships that govern modern life are affected. The interactions between the individual and the corporation, between the individual and the state, between one corporation and another, and between one sovereign government and another are today being profoundly altered.

Relationships between individuals are based on communication of one kind or another. The advent of the telegraph in business and the telephone in private life forever changed individual relationships by making it possible to communicate immediately over long distances. Like much new technology, when the telephone was new, even skilled politicians failed to grasp its importance. President Rutherford B. Hayes, after participating in an experimental telephone conversation between Washington and Philadelphia, commented: "That's an amazing invention, but who would ever want to use one of them." Today the president of the United States, sometimes to the distress of his cabinet officers, routinely picks up the phone to talk to world leaders wherever they may be—world leaders are no different in this respect than you and I. But the difference between this new form of diplomatic contact and the dispatch of a meticulously drafted note prepared by foreign policy professionals is immense (to say nothing of the records lost to history). Add to this the fact that decision makers sitting in the various situation and crisis-management rooms in the White House, the Department of State, and the Pentagon are often getting their information faster from the CNN News monitor than from official channels and the dimension of change becomes clear. While we are aware of this situation in a casual sort of way, those in a position to make policy must make a deliberate and powerful effort on a daily basis to realize the magnitude of change that has overtaken us. Their job is not to make some slight adjustment in their perception of the way the world's diplomatic games have been played for the last few hundred years but, rather, to understand an entirely new game, the rules of which are still being written. One new rule that is becoming more and more manifest is that technology has begun, in many instances, to bypass politics. As we have seen, the global financial markets have become the transmission belt for conveying the world's judgments about national economic policies. In a similar manner, the information technology that touches all of us each day has become the conduit for the myriad demands of citizens and consumers made to corporations and governments.

As hundreds of millions of people watched in awe and fascination, people took to the streets by the thousands in one Eastern European country after another and indeed in Moscow itself. No government, no matter how repressive or authoritarian, can over time stand in opposition to what Jefferson called "a decent respect to the opinions of mankind." No one should be naive enough to believe that the totalitarian powers of the world will give up easily, as the events in Tiananmen Square in China remind us all. But information is the virus that is carrying the powerful idea of freedom to the four corners of the world, and modern technology assures that sooner rather than later everyone on the planet will have heard the message.

Modern information technology is also driving nation-states toward cooperation with each other so that the world's work can get done. As news of the planet's problems, real or perceived, spreads, it becomes manifest that there are many problems that cannot be attacked effectively by any one nation-state, no matter how powerful. Events in one area may have huge consequences in another. Acid rain and the greenhouse effect are but two recent examples that are beyond the control of any single sovereign. The spread of information is being urged along by a host of new devices that appear almost daily.

The fax machine has become, in effect, the pamphleteer of the late twentieth century. In August 1991 the army of the USSR closed down all the radio and TV stations in Leningrad in an attempt to cut its cities off from news from the outside world. They overlooked the fax machines, and via fax, stories of the turmoil in Moscow were handed out on the barricades. These machines have joined audio- and videocassettes in spreading the word—good or bad—to an increasing percentage of the world's population. In addition to these devices, laptop personal computers are now tied together through myriad networks and thousands of computer "bulletin boards," and are employed to post and display news and information about everything from world events to dating services. The law of technology is the law of convergence, and just as consumer pressure has forced computer companies to find ways for differing computer systems to cooperate in order to solve problems, so nation-states are being forced to find ways to arrive at common standards. It is ironic that the aerospace industry—which is one of the most technologically advanced industries in the world—is the last to adopt the metric system (perhaps because of the influence of American companies).

> In a metric world, the aerospace industry remains the primary inch/pound holdout. . . . Even Europe's Airbus Industries builds aircraft for inch/pound tools. Pilots and air traffic controllers throughout the world report altitude in feet and distance in nautical miles, except in the Soviet Union and China.[5]

Despite this aberration, few would doubt that if Americans wish to compete in the global market that has gone metric for spare parts and materials, sooner or later these standards will be adopted.

As information technology brings the news of how others live and work, the pressures on any repressive government for freedom and human rights will soon grow intolerable because the world spotlight will be turned on abuses and citizens will demand their freedoms. While old power structures will resist this kind of outside interference, technology will render them obsolete. At the end of the day, technology will be seen to have brought effective pressure for reform. As the number of places on the planet grows where power really resides in the people, the world will become more, not less, complex. Democracy, which is simple in concept, is in practice an exceedingly complex system. We are not accustomed to living and operating in a kind of international democracy. We have instead lived our lives largely in the world dominated by two superpowers.

In our new world, both nation-states and corporations will have relatively less power. The frustration and inertia that sometimes accompany democracy will more and more affect the international community. In these circumstances, policymakers will have to display qualities of leadership rather than managerial skills in order to influence the outcome of our new arrangements. Democracy has always been an act of faith: It rests on the willingness of citizens to obey the unenforceable. Those of us who have lived in a democratic world will for some years have a huge advantage in our competition with the world.

Instant communication does not in and of itself create understanding. Thinking about the whole explosion of information and the way it is transmitted throughout the world, one might visualize a pyramid: At the bottom of the pyramid are data; the next layer up is information culled from all the data; the next layer is our experience. Each individual is the product to some extent of the velocity of his or her own experience, and it is information filtered through that experience that in the best of circumstances creates wisdom at the top of the pyramid. This process is by no means foreordained. Advanced technology does not produce wisdom; it does not change human nature; it does not make our problems go away. But it does and will speed us on our journey toward more human freedom. As Oliver Wendell Holmes, Jr., wrote, ". . . the best test of truth is the power of the thought to get itself accepted in the competition of the market. . . ." The new electronic infrastructure of the world turns the whole planet into a market for ideas, and the idea of freedom has proved again and again that it will win against any competing idea. We are thus witness to a true revolution; power really is moving to the people. Freedom as an individual attribute can be abused and debased, but as Lincoln put it: "Is there a better, or even an equal, hope in the world?" The age of information is helping to answer that question for the people of the world.

Notes

CHAPTER ONE. The Twilight of the Idols

1. For a full discussion, see George Gilder, *Microcosm* (New York: Simon & Schuster, 1989).
2. The twin organizations of the World Bank and the International Monetary Fund were conceived and funded by the Allies at a meeting in the New Hampshire village of Bretton Woods in July 1944. The bank was to promote economic development, and the IMF was to maintain orderly exchange rates to prevent competitive devaluations.
3. George Gilder, "The Emancipation of the CEO," *Chief Executive*, January/February 1988, p. 9.
4. Barbara W. Tuchman, *Practicing History* (New York: Ballantine Books, 1982), p. 250.

CHAPTER TWO. A New Source of Wealth

1. Conversation with Donald Barnett, March 31, 1990. Much of the information about modern steel making incorporated in this chapter comes from conversations with Barnett or from two of his books: *Steel: Upheaval in a Basic Industry* (Cambridge: Ballinger, 1983); and (coauthored with Robert Crandall) *Up from the Ashes: The Rise of the Steel Minimill in the United States* (Washington, D.C.: Brookings Institution, 1986). See also *The Competitive Status of the U.S. Steel Industry* (Washington, D.C.: National Academy Press, 1985).
2. *The Competitive Status of the U.S. Steel Industry*, A Study

of the Influences of Technology in Determining International Competitive Advantages, National Research Council (Washington, D.C.: National Academy Press, 1985), p. 2.

3. Tom Redburn and James Flanigan, "U.S. Firms Regain Competitive Edge," *Los Angeles Times*, 2 August 1987.

4. Alan Greenspan, "Goods Shrink and Trade Grows," *Wall Street Journal*, 24 October 1988.

5. Peter F. Drucker, *The New Realities* (New York: Harper & Row, 1989), p. 122.

6. Ibid., p. 123.

7. Cited by Henry W. Spiegal in *The Growth of American Economic Thought* (Durham, N.C.: Duke University Press, 1991).

8. Peter Drucker has stated this many times, but first in *The Age of Discontinuity* (New York: Harper & Row, 1969).

CHAPTER THREE. **THE GLOBAL CONVERSATION**

1. Robert J. Saunders, Jeremy J. Warford, and Bjorn Wellenius, *Telecommunications and Economic Development* (Baltimore: John Hopkins University Press for the World Bank, 1983), p. 19.

2. Federal Reserve Bank of New York, *Summary of Results of U.S. Foreign Exchange Market Survey Conducted in April 1989*, Released September 13, 1989.

3. E. T. Mottram, "First Transatlantic Telephone Cable," *Bell Laboratories Record*, February 1957, pp. 41–47.

4. Bruce Dougherty, Presentation to Tandem Computers board of directors, 1990.

5. Kenneth Dam, "The Global Electronic Market," Paper presented at the IIC Conference, Washington, D.C., 1988.

6. Ibid.

7. *Industry Basics* (Washington, D.C.: North American Telecommunications Association, 1986), pp. 17–19.

8. Oswald H. and Gladys D. Ganley, *Inform or Control*, 2nd

ed. (Norwood, N.J.: Ablex Publishing Corp., 1989), p. 59.

9. Stuart H. Loory, "News from the Global Village," *Gannett Center Journal*, Fall 1989, p. 167.

10. Timothy Garton Ash, *The Magic Lantern* (New York: Random House, 1990), p. 94.

11. For an excellent discussion of the worldwide spread of VCRs and the political implications thereof, see Gladys and Oswald Ganley, *Global Political Fallout, The VCR's First Decade* (Norwood, N.J.: Ablex, 1987), p. 4.

12. For an informative study of the current state of Soviet communications and the implications of the former Soviet government's commitment to change, see Wilson P. Dizard and S. Blake Swensrud, *Gorbachev's Information Revolution*, Center for Strategic and International Studies (Boulder, Colo.: Westview Press, 1987).

13. Ash, *Magic Lantern*, p. 138.

14. Peter Drucker, *The New Realities* (New York: Harper & Row, 1989), p. 190.

CHAPTER FOUR. **T**HE **I**NFORMATION **S**TANDARD

1. F. A. Hayek, *Denationalisation of Money* (London: Institute of Economic Affairs, 1976), p. 28.

2. Testimony given on May 16, 1961 before the Subcommittee on International Exchange and Payments of the Joint Economic Committee, Congress of the United States.

3. Norris Johnson, *Eurodollars in the New International Money Market*, published by First National City Bank, (New York, 1964).

4. *New York Times*, 26 March 1990, p. 1.

CHAPTER FIVE. **T**HE **E**ND OF THE **T**RADE

1. Martin Wolf, Briefing paper for Manhattan Institute presented on April 24, 1989.

2. F. A. Hayek, *The Fatal Conceit* (Chicago: University of Chicago Press, 1988), p. 77.

3. C. W. Cole, *Colbert and a Century of French Mercantilism* (New York: Columbia University Press, 1939), p. 337.

4. Robert F. Heibroner, ed., *The Essential Adam Smith*, (New York: W. W. Norton, 1986), p. 171.

5. Richard I. Kirkland, Jr., "Entering a New Age of Boundless Competition," *Fortune*, 14 March 1988, p. 41.

6. *Transnational Corporations in World Development: Trends and Prospects* (New York: United Nations Center on Transnational Corporations, United Nations, 1988), p. 20.

7. *Economic Report of the President* (Washington, D.C.: U. S. Government Printing Office, January 1989), p. 424.

8. Kirkland, "Boundless Competition," p. 17.

9. *New York Times*, Report of numbers released by central banks, 14 September 1989.

10. Saul Hansell, "The Wild, Wired World of Electronic Exchanges," *Institutional Investor*, September 1989, p. 91.

11. Information from IBM. A letter dated November 10, 1989, signed by D. S. Hager.

12. Kirkland, "Boundless Competition," p. 41.

13. Quoted in Kirkland, "Boundless Competition," p. 40.

14. Ibid., p. 40.

15. Kenich Ohmae, *The Borderless World* (New York: HarperBusiness, 1990), p. 141.

16. Information from an article by Charles R. Morris, "The Coming Global Boom," *Atlantic Monthly*, October 1989.

17. *Transnational Corporations*, p. 56. In some cases these alliances included some aspects of the traditional joint venture, as many alliances do.

CHAPTER SIX. **WHERE WE STAND**

1. Fernand Braudel, *The Structures of Everyday Life* (New York: Harper & Row, 1981), p. 34.

2. For a complete history of the measurement of time see: Daniel Boorstin, *The Discoverers* (New York, Random House, 1983).
3. Murray Weidenbaum, "Geopolitics and Geoeconomics: Systems Out of Sync," *Directors and Boards*, 14: no. 4 (September 1990).
4. George Stigler, *The Economist as Preacher* (Chicago: University of Chicago Press, 1990), p. 6.
5. For complete figures see *Economic Report of the President* (Washington, D.C.: U.S. Government Printing Office, 1988).
6. *Financial Times*, London, 9 January 1989.
7. Figures supplied by Frank Metz, chief financial officer of IBM.

CHAPTER SEVEN. **SERENDIPITY, INC.**

1. Poul Anderson, *Satan's World* (New York: Berkley Publishing Group, 1989).
2. James R. Beniger, *The Control Revolution* (Cambridge, Mass.: Harvard University Press, 1986), p. 224.
3. Ibid., pp. 224–25.
4. Ibid., p. 243.
5. Ibid., pp. 393, 398.
6. Peter F. Drucker, *The New Realities* (New York: Harper & Row, 1989), p. 212.
7. Shoshana Zuboff, *In the Age of the Smart Machine* (New York: Basic Books, 1988), p. 252.
8. Ibid., p. 252.
9. Ibid., p. 280.
10. Ibid., p. 290.
11. Ibid., p. 291.

CHAPTER EIGHT. **BORDERS ARE NOT BOUNDARIES**

1. E. J. Hobsbawm, *Nations and Nationalism Since 1780* (New York: Cambridge University Press, 1990), pp. 174–75.
2. Ithiel de Sola Pool, *Technologies Without Boundaries* (Cambridge: Harvard University Press, 1990), p. 73.
3. Richard D. Brown, *Knowledge Is Power* (New York: Oxford University Press, 1989), p. 279.
4. *New York Times* vs. *United States*, 1971, U.S.S.C.
5. Jeane J. Kirkpatrick, *The Withering Away of the Totalitarian State* (Washington, D.C.: The AEI Press, 1990), p. 273.
6. Rupert Murdoch, MacTaggart Lecture, August 25, 1989.
7. Ibid.
8. Ibid.
9. Blanca Riemer and Karen Wolman, *Business Week*, 27 March 1989, pp. 46–47.
10. *Yearbook of International Organizations*, 8th ed. (New Providence, N.J.: K. G. Saur, 1990/91).
11. Oswald H. and Gladys D. Ganley, *To Inform or to Control?* 2nd ed. (Norwood, N.J.: Ablex Publishing Co., 1989).
12. Kenichi Ohmae, "Managing in a Borderless World," *Harvard Business Review*, May–June 1989, p. 153.
13. See Daniel Boorstin, *The Image: A Guide to Pseudo-Events in America* (New York: Atheneum, 1962).
14. Fernand Braudel, *The Wheels of Commerce* (New York: Harper & Row, 1982), p. 515.
15. Michael J. O'Neill, *Terrorist Spectaculars* (New York: Twentieth Century Fund, 1986, p. 53.
16. Gladys and Oswald H. Ganley, *Global Political Fallout*, p. 4.
17. Stuart H. Loory, "News From the Global Village," *Gannett Center Journal*, Fall 1989, p. 169.

CHAPTER NINE. **THE GREAT EQUALIZER**

1. David Kahn, *The Code Breakers* (New York: Macmillan, 1967), p. 82.
2. Barbara Tuchman, *The First Salute* (New York: Ballantine, 1988), p. 232.
3. David Kahn, *The Code Breakers*, p. 162.
4. Ibid., p. 510.
5. Alan Palmer, *An Encyclopedia of Napoleon's Europe* (New York: St. Martin's Press, 1984), p. 23.
6. *Aviation Week & Space Technology*, 31 July 1989, pp. 55–67.
7. Michael Fitzpatrick, "A Case Study in Weapons Acquisition: The Sidewinder Air to Air Missile," *Journal of International Affairs*, Summer 1985, p. 175.
8. Gladys D. and Oswald H. Ganley, *To Inform or to Control?* (Norwood, N.J.: Ablex Publishing Co., 1989), p. 231.
9. Ibid., p. 234.
10. A Paper by the Standoff Weapons Panel, Offense-Defense Working Group, submitted to the Commission on Integrated Long-Term Strategy, October 1988, p. 1.
11. Ibid., p. 2.
12. Ibid.
13. Scott A. Boorman and Paul R. Levitt, "Deadly Bugs," *Sunday* (*Chicago Tribune* magazine), 3 May 1987, section 10.
14. Scott Boorman and Paul Levitt, "Software Warfare and Algorithm Sabotage," *Signal*, May 1988.
15. Ibid.
16. For the full story, see Clifford Stoll, *The Cuckoo's Egg* (New York: Doubleday, 1989).
17. Ibid., p. 303.
18. James Bamford, *The Puzzle Palace* (New York: Penguin Books, 1983), p. 448.
19. Winston S. Churchill, "The Wizard War," chap. 4 in *Their Finest Hour* (Boston: Houghton Mifflin, 1949), p. 381.

CHAPTER TEN. **POWER TO THE PEOPLE**

1. William Safire, *Safire's Political Dictionary* (New York: Ballantine Books, 1980), p. 560.
2. Christopher Cerf and Victor Navasky, *The Experts Speak* (New York: Pantheon Books, 1984), p. 207.
3. Agnes Rogers and Frederick Lewis Allen, *I Remember Distinctly* (New York: Harper Brothers, 1947), p. 37.
4. Ibid., p. 36.
5. *Aviation Week & Space Technology*, November 1989, p. 7.

INDEX

ABOUT THE AUTHOR

WALTER B. WRISTON retired as chairman and chief executive officer of Citicorp and its principal subsidiary, Citibank, N.A., on September 1, 1984, after having served as chief executive officer for seventeen years and in various other positions with the company for thirty-eight years.

Mr. Wriston was born in Middletown, Connecticut, on August 3, 1919, and graduated from Wesleyan University and the Fletcher School of Law and Diplomacy at Tufts University. Following a year's service as a U.S. State Department officer and a four-year tour with the U.S. Army during World War II, Mr. Wriston joined Citibank in 1946 as a junior inspector in the Comptroller's Division.

He was assigned to the National Division in 1949 and served in the division's Canadian and Transportation districts for seven years, becoming an assistant cashier in 1950, an assistant vice president in 1952, and a vice president in 1954.

Mr. Wriston joined the bank's Overseas Division in 1956, heading the European District for three years, and was named a senior vice president in 1958. The following year he was made head of the Overseas Division and was appointed executive vice president in 1960. Mr. Wriston became president and chief executive officer of the bank in 1967 and of the corporation when it was formed in 1968. He became chairman in 1970.

Mr. Wriston is a director of the General Electric Company, the Chubb Corporation, Bechtel Investments, Inc., Sequoia Ventures, Inc., Tandem Computers, Inc., United Meridian Corporation, and ICOS Corporation. He was chairman of President Ronald Reagan's Economic Policy Advisory Board, a member and former chairman of the Business Council, and a former co-chairman and policy committee member of the Business Roundtable. He is a trustee of the American Enterprise Institute and the Manhattan Institute for Policy Research, a member of the

Board of Visitors of the Fletcher School of Law and Diplomacy, and a life governor of New York Hospital.

Mr. Wriston's first book, *Risk and Other Four-Letter Words*, a collection of essays, was published by Harper & Row in 1986.

Mr. Wriston married the former Kathryn Ann Dineen in March 1968. His first wife, the former Barbara Brengle, died in 1966. He has one daughter, Catherine W. (Mrs. Richard M.) Quintal, and lives in New York City.